A Constitutional Conversation

A Constitutional Conversation

Letters from an
Ohio Farmer

Ashbrook Press

Library of Congress Cataloging-in-Publication Data

A Constitutional Conversation: Letters from an Ohio Farmer;
by An Ohio Farmer

p.   cm.
Includes Index
1. United States—Politics and government.

ISBN 978-1-878802-27-9 (pbk.)

Ashbrook Center at Ashland University
401 College Avenue
Ashland, Ohio 44805
www.ashbrook.org

Contents

Preface

The American people have started a historic conversation – about the foundations, purposes, and scope of our government. In a spontaneous movement they rose to challenge long-established orthodoxies, and a sustained exertion of their sovereign power is changing the direction in which the country is heading. The movement began with no headquarters, no recognized leader, and no agreed upon platform. Thousands of independent groups of private citizens gathered in thousands of public squares across the land. Through all the diverse ideas expressed in these gatherings, one theme shone clearly: the federal government has, over the last several decades, stepped further and further outside the bounds of the Constitution.

How did our government get to this point? What would constitutional government look like? What paths are available to the people and their representatives for returning to constitutional self-government? These and related questions were taken up in a series of weekly letters sent to the 112th Congress over the past year, and collected here, as a humble contribution to this American conversation – a constitutional conversation in the broadest sense. The letters continue and can be read weekly at: www.ohiofarmer.org.

The Ohio Farmer is not one person, but a group of citizens seeking to preserve constitutional self-government in America. The Farmer's letters are written in the tradition of the Federalists and Antifederalists in the American founding who wrote newspaper articles debating the new form of government proposed in the Constitution of 1787. They wrote using pen names such as Publius, or Federal Farmer, or American Citizen, to allow their arguments to speak for themselves and be judged on their own merits. The letters from the Ohio Farmer are offered in the same spirit.

The Ohio Farmer is a project of the Ashbrook Center. The various authors who compose each letter from the Ohio Farmer are partisans in one sense: they are partisans of the constitutional self-government they regard as America's greatest gift to the world. The Ohio Farmer is not primarily concerned with immediate policy questions, though he necessarily discusses them; he hopes to refine and enlarge the public's view of the larger political principles implicit in our policy debates. He is a friend to all who love this country and wish it well; he is searching for that common ground that can unite all reasonable parties who wish to maintain America's glorious tradition of constitutional self-government.

Constitution Day, 2011

A Constitutional Conversation

No. 1

A Constitutional Conversation
February 10, 2011

To the Members of the 112th Congress:

I write in all humility as your sovereign – I mean as one of the millions of American citizens who together bear the ultimate responsibility for this land of freedom that you and we love. I write as your new session gets under way because I am convinced that this is a pivotal moment in our country's history, when our choices and yours hold tremendous consequences for America's future, for our children and grandchildren.

To begin your session, newly elected Republican members put the Constitution in the forefront of Congress's deliberations – scheduling an unprecedented reading of the Constitution on the floor of the House and proposing that every bill be required to cite constitutional authority for its enactment. Some Democrats and some in the media criticized these actions. I would like to think that the actions and the criticism may be hopeful signs, that they may mark the beginning of a conversation in the country that is overdue – a long, probing conversation among friends, with no holds barred.

The people should be active participants in this conversation. In earlier fateful moments in the life of the country – the Revolution, the debate over the Constitution, the Civil War and Reconstruction, the New Deal, the Civil Rights Era – the nation rose in serious and sustained argument about the foundations, purposes, scope, and form of our government. It seems to me that this is just the kind of conversation – a constitutional conversation in the broadest sense – that the country needs to have today. This is the first in a series of essays modestly hoping to contribute to this distinctly American conversation.

Who is the Ohio Farmer? He is not one person. In the manner of *The Federalist Papers* back in 1787-88, the Ohio Farmer letters will be written singly and jointly by different concerned citizens who would like their arguments to speak for themselves and to be judged on their merits. Like

Publius, we candidly avow our political sympathies: We are partisans of the Constitution. But what does that mean? It is my hope in forthcoming letters to answer that question thoroughly.

To begin: it seems to me that one of the great errors of recent decades is the supposition that constitutional questions are matters only for lawyers and judges to decide. The Constitution begins with "We, the people," not "We, the judges." It belongs to all the people, and to all three branches of government. Thinking about the Constitution is a responsibility of our *citizenship* as it is of your *statesmanship*.

So, as you go about your business as members of Congress, it seems altogether fitting and proper not only to show reverence for the Constitution – or to criticize such shows of reverence, if you think that better serves the Constitution – but to express your own constitutional views as they bear upon your business – our business – and to argue in public on behalf of those views. This would seem to be fully in keeping with the oath you recently took to support and defend the Constitution, an oath I expect you will take with solemn seriousness, and in honor of which you will daily strive to make your conduct as legislators conform to the limitations and principles of the Constitution, as you understand them.

I am inclined to think that the best hope right now for developing a fruitful constitutional deliberation in the country arises from the political spirit of the citizenry that led to the historic recent elections. In those elections we expressed, I think, the greatest human power active in the world today, a power handed down to us – secured for us in revolution, preserved for us through civil war and world wars – through the generations since 1776. It is our constitutional responsibility to speak with such power – a power derivative from a source prior even to the Constitution, our fundamental right of revolution – and it is our constant prayer that our wisdom will somehow equal our authority. I think the freedom of this country, and the cause of freedom itself, depends on this prayer being favorably answered.

But, of course, we are not wise. As everyone has seen, we were roused in a historic way in these recent elections. In large numbers, we tore ourselves away from the private concerns of family and work to go into the public square, to join our neighbors in giving hours and days to the affairs we hold in common, to the common good of the country. But we brought our human and American limits and imperfections to these elections, as to all others.

We acted in some ways uncertainly and ambiguously and incompletely. We spoke with many millions of voices in several hundreds of separate elections just at the national level. And of course our minds will change as we see events unfolding and decisions being made in the coming months and years. That seems to be the nature of the sovereign you serve – not easy to please, often not easy to understand. But nonetheless the one you answer to and whose cool and deliberate sense you seek to represent.

So what did we mean in this election? What do we hope for from you? What do we have a right to expect from you? What does your and our constitutional duty require of us? In the course of these essays, which will appear weekly or with greater frequency as circumstances permit, I hope to consider conversationally these questions and the whole range of questions of mutual interest to sovereign citizens and their elected representatives.

But let me say again that I write in humility – humbled because the honor of being sovereign over this dear country is so great and the responsibility so momentous; humbled by my own limitations, limitations I and my fellow citizens readily acknowledge even while speaking, as we are bound to do, with sovereign gravity.

OHIO FARMER

No. 2

An Experiment in Self-Government
February 17, 2011

To the Members of the 112th Congress:

I wrote in the last letter about the sovereignty of the people and about the oaths you take as members of Congress to uphold the Constitution. Both seem to me to be related in a beautiful way to the American experiment in self-government.

Whenever I happen to think about it, I can't help feeling a fresh sense of wonder, and then of gratitude, that the American people, upon achieving sovereign independence and proclaiming to the world their right to govern themselves, submitted their sovereign power to a Constitution, which was at once their creation and the Supreme Law over them. This great political act reflected, I think, our recognition that the people's sovereign power is itself subject to what Thomas Jefferson called "the great principles of right and wrong." As Jefferson put it, it was not an "elective despotism" we fought for; we seemed to understand that if our right to self-government was to lead to good government, we must establish conditions under which our authoritative consent might become reflection and deliberation – conditions for drawing out from our sovereign selves what Publius called "the cool and deliberate sense of the community." To form ourselves into a community in which, in Madison's word, "Reason" might rule, we formed ourselves into a constitutional people. We devised for ourselves constitutional ways of constructing and shaping the authoritative consent of the people into constitutional deliberations by which we would be governed.

Think what a people we must already have been, to be determined and able to do such a thing. When the American revolutionaries and Founders looked back on the history of popular governments in the world (and they were avid students of that history), they beheld scene upon scene of turbulence and instability, of violent agitation between the extremes of anarchy and tyranny. So terrible was the picture, as Publius said, that it gave advocates of despotism an argument against free government altogether. Nonetheless, because of what they called their "honorable determination...to rest all our political experiments on the capacity of mankind for self-government," the American Revolutionaries insisted that American government would be founded on the "consent of the governed." In fact, as the Founders knew, the proud American people would not accept any other form of government.

But this would have been a false pride, it would have been not an honorable but a foolish determination, if the American people did not possess the capacity for self-government they generously claimed for mankind. But they proved themselves not only determined to establish a government based on consent, but capable, in Benjamin Franklin's famous phrase, of "keep[ing] it." They proved themselves not only to have the pride to insist on freedom, but the virtues necessary to do honor to it (may this always be the case). In subjecting themselves to the Constitution as they did, they proved themselves already to possess a constitution, in their souls – the constitution of a free people, without which the written Constitution would be useless parchment.

This constitution in our American souls expressed itself in a small way recently in our expectation and gratification that members of Congress should take an oath to uphold the Constitution. This is an oath of fidelity to the Constitution, and not to us, the people. Our high regard for this oath, it seems to me, is the sovereign people's way of telling our representatives that we expect you to be somewhat independent of us, that we think good government depends upon it. Those who originally conceived this Constitution said in many different ways that you would do your job well by remaining true to the Constitution, even when some people – I mean, us – clamored for you to do otherwise. In such moments, we count on you to "refine and enlarge" the public's view with your constitutional deliberations. Your oath opens a slight but decisive space between the people and their representatives, in which you can exercise your constitutional judgment in carrying out your lawmaking duties. Of course, you will often disagree among yourselves about what your duty to the Constitution requires of you. But articulating those differences will benefit all of us by contributing to a constitutional politics which will be the most reliable source of enduring sound policy. If we are as good as we claim to be, you will earn our respect, and our vote, when you respect the

Constitution and help us to do the same, even despite what we sometimes might think is our contrary interest.

OHIO FARMER

No. 3

_____

Civility and Powers
March 8, 2011

To the Members of the 112th Congress:

"Civility" has been a word to conjure with for the past few weeks. Since the terrible killings and woundings in Tucson, Americans could hardly open a newspaper or turn on a television without someone shouting at us most uncivilly in the name of civility. In the name of making us all friends, "civility" is wielded as a cudgel would be wielded against hated enemies. The word is deployed as a weapon, the way "bipartisanship" has sometimes been deployed in the service of the most narrow and unseemly partisanship.

Citizens' eyes roll and glaze over at such unserious and trumped up scolding. But civility is a serious theme. We want civility in our civil discourse because, in the language of the Founders, we want reason and not passion to govern our affairs. We insist that we will be ruled by the consent of the people, and we are aware at the same time that the people can become a mob. And so, as the last letter observed, we have devised "constitutional ways of constructing and shaping the authoritative consent of the people" so that the "cool and deliberate sense of the community" might prevail in our political deliberations.

Among the constitutional devices intended to help achieve this difficult and desirable result, separation of powers ranks high. This idea, "that the legislative, executive and judiciary departments ought to be separate and distinct," is (let us hope!) familiar to every American eighth grader; let us even be so immodest as to say that it is an essential American contribution to the advancement of constitutional governance. Separation of powers was so important to the Founders that they thought, in James Madison's words, that "[t]he accumulation of all powers legislative, executive and judiciary in the same hands … may justly be pronounced the very definition of tyranny." But I won't rehearse here what (I trust) we all have learned on the subject from fondly remembered grammar school teachers.

In the spirit of renewed attention to the Constitution that distinguishes this Congress, I will hope merely to observe something that may not be quite so obvious and may have a bearing on Congress's response to current challenges. Put simply, in our Constitution the branches are separate, but they are not equal: the vast preponderance of federal authority is delegated to Congress, which is without question the preeminent branch under the Constitution. One reason this may not be as obvious as it should be just by reading the Constitution is that, over the last 50 years, the separation of powers has tilted a bit out of constitutional balance. The presidential and judicial branches have become assertive and bold in articulating the national agenda, and Congress has largely deferred to this (or to the bureaucracy), sometimes in an effort to avoid difficult or potentially unpopular actions. Think of the fact that we call the recent historic elections "midterm" elections, as if Congress is a sideshow and the Presidency is the main event.

In our Constitution, Congress is the main event, and our separation of powers will serve us better if Congress is not as deferential as it has become accustomed to being (whether to the executive, the judiciary, or the bureaucracy). Let Congress reassert the lawmaking preeminence and responsibility intended for it in the Constitution – initiating constitutional conversations, setting out an agenda which is not necessarily the President's or the Court's, overturning what the members may consider to be the wayward actions of the other branches – and our constitutional deliberations as a whole will benefit.

I hasten to add, lest "irrational exuberance" seize the day, that when Congress acts boldly and takes the legislative initiative the Constitution intends for it to take, members should do so on behalf of their constitutional duty and not for mere party advantage, and they (and we) should hope and expect to find that the executive branch and the judiciary will rise to resist any assertions that seem to them unacceptable, behaving just as is intended in the Constitutional design. This proper functioning of the separation of powers (aided by the checks and balances within Congress) is meant to impede the misuse of Congressional power. We and Congress will display a kind of constitutional wisdom and patience, I think, if we recognize that the power to resist misuses of Congressional power is also a power that might on occasion thwart the necessary and proper uses of Congressional power.

More generally speaking, if separation of powers is designed to impede the rash introduction of radical change, it also has the effect of making it difficult to undo such change. If this Congress thinks it is its duty to do just that, let it act and give its reasons. It will meet resistance, and we all should expect that reasons will be given in turn. This is our Constitution at work. Citizens should anticipate serious argument, not just about policies, but about rights and duties, about the powers of government and limitations on those powers. We should all learn from this, and all of this, of course, takes time. And if our elected representatives can't sort it out, then the people, through the ballot box, will speak again, and a new constitutional deliberation, possibly with different participants, will begin.

A final word: No constitutional devices like separation of powers – none of these "inventions of prudence," as Publius called them – will bring civility or cool and deliberate reflection from a nation of savages. So our broader constitutional deliberations should include not just civility but all the virtues, capacities, and principles that must shape the character of a people if they mean, as we do mean, to be self-governing. Among the themes to include in these deliberations is the civic friendship, the care for one another, even in our millions, that could not be missed when the news of the Tucson tragedies spread across the land.

OHIO FARMER

No. 4

Reconstitutionalizing America

March 15, 2011

To the Members of the 112th Congress:

To bring American government back within the bounds of the Constitution – to reconstitutionalize it – will be no easy or simple task. How dismissive of the Constitution our government has become was memorably expressed by then Speaker of the House, Nancy Pelosi, in two widely quoted remarks about the health care bill that ultimately became the Patient Protection and Affordable Care Act (PPACA), whose constitutionality is seriously in dispute right now. It is worth recalling her words, because they are a surface expression of an attitude toward our politics that is deeply entrenched and must be replaced by a very different attitude if we are to recover constitutional self-government. In October 2009 when a reporter from CNSNews.com asked, "Where specifically does the Constitution grant Congress the authority to enact an individual health insurance mandate?" Pelosi replied, "Are you serious? Are you serious?" Then in a March 2010 speech, Pelosi said, "We have to pass the bill so you can find out what's in it."

Her rhetorical question – "Are you serious?" – was, of course, meant not to begin but to end conversation. Such contemptuous dismissal of citizens' serious concern about constitutionality made many voters indignant last November, and they carried their well justified indignation with them to the ballot box. The arrogant contempt continued in the sniffing dismissals that greeted the new Congress's show of respect for the Constitution. This arrogance comes from a belief that is held to be unquestionable. This is the belief that the New Deal irrevocably transformed America into a country whose central government has the authority to address any social or economic problem, and to mandate or proscribe any individual conduct plausibly related to alleviating that problem. To the former Speaker and those who agree with her, it is preposterous – mind-boggling – that any 21st century American should presume to question this article of faith. The same arrogant incredulity struts and postures angrily in Wisconsin and Ohio and other states where public employee unions and their advocates in the media assert a right to collective bargaining that is somehow supposed to be regarded as sacred and beyond question. Whatever citizens may think of the merits of the question, the arrogance of such assertions sticks in the craw of those who cherish self-government.

Pelosi's second statement acknowledges that in this post-New Deal America, when Congress does something, it's not really Congress that does it. We have to pass a bill to find out what's in it because what's "in" it resides nowhere in the language of the legislation, but in the rulings and regulations that will be handed down, months and years after the bill-signing ceremony, by administrative agencies empowered by Congress to make all the practical policy determinations. What one New Dealer advocated in 1937 has come to pass – every important law enacted by Congress is really "a declaration of war, so that the essence of the program is in the gradual unfolding of the plan in actual administration." In PPACA's declaration of war on the problem of people being uninsured, under-insured, or over-insured, it creates 159 new federal entities to devise and execute a battle plan.

Representative Pelosi is right about the way America is governed now: The federal government can do just about any*thing* it wants, and can do it just about any *way* it wants. It can do this because, in the course of the last two generations, the federal government has assumed responsibility for the social and economic well-being of every American. This required the creation of programs for managing in minute detail all the social and economic relations between all the different members and segments of American society – employers and employees, producers and consumers, doctors and patients, husbands and wives, parents and children, and on and on. Because Congress cannot possibly write legislation governing so many details of so many interactions, it must outsource rule-making to boards, agencies and commissions, such as the Elder Justice Coordinating Council or the Cures Acceleration Network created in PPACA.

As the New Deal was gathering steam the Supreme Court held, in 1935, that such "delegation run riot" violated the Constitution's assignment of legislative power to Congress. That is, the Constitution does not permit Congress to delegate its powers to any other governmental entity.

The Court has never explicitly overturned that decision, though it has implicitly negated it over the subsequent 76 years by acquiescing as Congress plunged ahead in riotous delegation. When Congress delegates real governance in this way to agencies not answerable to the American people, it creates the conditions for lawless policy, subjecting every detail of American life to regulators bound by nothing but their own will.

In the reading of the Constitution with which the newly elected House of Representatives began its first session, one hopes that every member gave full attention to Article I, Section 1: "All legislative powers herein granted shall be vested in a Congress of the United States." Supreme Court justice Hugo Black famously wrote about the First Amendment that "'No law' means *no law*." By the same token, we cannot reconstitutionalize American government until jurists, legislators, and citizens begin to insist, "'All legislative powers' means *all legislative powers*."

This reconstitutionalization would have been assisted if the House had also sat for a reading of the Declaration of Independence, especially the part about governments "deriving their just powers from the consent of the governed." The 62nd *Federalist* warned us against the sort of hyperactive government needed to secure every citizen's socioeconomic well-being: "It will be of little avail to the people, that the laws are made by men of their own choice, if the laws be so voluminous that they cannot be read, or so incoherent that they cannot be understood; if they be repealed or revised before they are promulgated, or undergo such incessant changes that no man, who knows what the law is to-day, can guess what it will be tomorrow." The predicament becomes much worse when the blizzard of edicts is issued, not by "men of our own choice," but by appointed and usually life-tenured civil servants who cannot be removed or rebuked by mere citizens. This arrangement dilutes and attenuates the consent of the governed so severely that it deprives the government of what the Founders considered the only source of legitimate power. We should bend our efforts to recovering the full range and authority of the constitutional consent from which the just powers of government are derived.

OHIO FARMER

No. 5

A Boundless Field of Power
March 22, 2011

To the Members of the 112th Congress:

Do the powers granted by the Constitution authorize the federal government to require private citizens to purchase health insurance policies? Leading progressive politicians and intellectuals dismiss this question as not serious – in their view the question is closed, irrevocably settled by the triumph of the New Deal. Nonetheless, the nation is taking it seriously, and is engaged in a historic constitutional deliberation on the question.

This individual mandate, as it has come to be called, is widely considered to be crucial to the Patient Protection and Affordable Care Act (PPACA), the "Obamacare" law enacted in 2010. It is considered crucial because the law prohibits health insurance companies from refusing to sell policies to people on the basis of pre-existing medical conditions, and from imposing a lifetime cap on the dollar amount of reimbursements. In light of these provisions, it is reasonable to expect that without an individual mandate, many people will respond to Obamacare's incentives by waiting until they're seriously ill to buy insurance. No health insurance company could survive if forced to operate under that arrangement, in the same way no property insurance company could survive if its customers could wait until their houses were on fire to buy homeowner's policies.

As part of our constitutional deliberations, lawsuits have been filed against PPACA, with mixed results; some federal judges have upheld the constitutionality of the individual mandate, and others have deemed it unconstitutional. While the question makes its uncertain way to the Supreme Court, American citizens who are not necessarily judges, scholars or lawyers continue to wrestle with it as a matter of politics, in light of the larger question: What can the federal government do under the Constitution, and what can't it do?

America has an instructive history of considering this question. The first big fight over it concerned the federal power to create a Bank of the United States. When President George Washington's Secretary of the Treasury, Alexander Hamilton, proposed such a bank in 1791, Secretary of State Thomas Jefferson objected. He contended that because the power to create a bank was "not among the powers specially enumerated" in the Constitution, its establishment would be "a single step beyond the boundaries" drawn around the federal government, which would lead it to "take possession of a boundless field of power, no longer susceptible of any definition." Hamilton's position was that for each power the Constitution confers on the government it also and necessarily confers "a right to employ all the means requisite and fairly applicable to the attainment of the ends of such power," unless the Constitution specifically denies a particular exercise of power to the federal government. Hamilton's argument persuaded Washington to sign rather than veto the bill creating a Bank of the United States.

Twenty-eight years later, Hamilton's and Washington's view was upheld in the famous Supreme Court decision, *McCulloch vs. Maryland* (1819). As Chief Justice John Marshall wrote for the Court: "If the end be legitimate, and within the scope of the Constitution, all the means which are appropriate, which are plainly adapted to that end, and which are not prohibited, may constitutionally be employed to carry it into effect." But Marshall also wrote that the government of the United States "is acknowledged by all to be one of enumerated powers," and the "question respecting the extent of the powers actually granted is perpetually arising, and will probably continue to arise so long as our system shall exist."

The debate over Obamacare shows that, as Justice Marshall expected, the question about where to draw the line between legitimate and illegitimate exercises of federal authority is still very much alive in the American constitutional conversation. Jefferson, so to speak, continues to argue with Hamilton. Those who challenge the constitutionality of the law seem concerned, among other things, at the "boundless field of power" Congress seems to claim when it asserts a power to compel all Americans to enter into whatever private economic relationships Congress deems convenient to its purposes. Federal district court judge Roger Vinson expressed some of this concern in the Florida case, *State of Florida v. United States Department of Health and Human Services*, where he wrote that "Never before has Congress required that everyone buy a product from a private company (essentially for life) just for being alive and residing in the United States."

It is true, as I remarked in my last letter, that with the entrenching and expanding of the New Deal and the Great Society, America has reached a point where "the federal government can do just about any*thing* it wants, and can do it just about any *way* it wants." Our progressive politicians and intellectuals insist that this condition is irreversible – beyond serious question. The movement of American politics over the past two years seems to be proving that this is not the case. And so the progressive insistence that the question is closed gets louder and more desperate. Just opening the question is a significant achievement, though it leaves much statesman's work still to do – as Hamilton and Jefferson teach us. We can learn much from both of them as we continue to recover the kind of constitutional reasoning these letters hope to help restore to governing in our country.

OHIO FARMER

No. 6

Capacities of Mankind
March 29, 2011

To the Members of the 112th Congress:

In recent weeks, the course of human events – from Tunisia, to Libya, to Egypt, to Syria – reminds Americans once again that tyranny is common in the world, that it is hard to remove, and that it is even harder to replace it with freedom and good government. We Americans, of every political stripe, generally like to consider ourselves enemies of tyranny and friends of freedom in the world. Of course, we have lots of debates among ourselves (and with others) about what this means and what this requires of American foreign policy. These debates have been rekindled lately, and I take this occasion to recollect that America came into existence by overthrowing a tyranny and that we have had our own struggles replacing it with freedom and good government.

Our success in these struggles – to the extent that we have met with success – is due to moral and political habits and dispositions that arise from principles that must be learned. These principles and dispositions are the most essential conditions of freedom. Everything else is secondary. Without them, you might exchange an unpopular for a popular tyranny, an incompetent and destitute tyranny for a competent and wealthy one. But you will never have free government.

America began its experiment in freedom with what has become and will forever remain the most characteristic and defining American affirmation: "We hold these truths to be self-evident, that all men are created equal, that they are endowed by their creator with certain inalienable rights." The truth of human equality and liberty was asserted against all tyrannies – whether of race, class, or religion, one, few, or many.

That men throughout history tyrannized one another in an infinite variety of ways was not proof to the American Founders that human beings do not possess equal rights by nature – rather it was proof of how rare and difficult a thing it is to secure them. It is proof of the philosophic rigor, the moral discipline, the political sagacity, and the beneficence of opportunity that are required for reflection and free choice to prevail over ignorance, prejudice, accident, and force.

Proclaiming that all men everywhere and at all times possess by nature equal rights to life, liberty, and the pursuit of happiness, the American Founders undertook the historic effort to secure these rights, so far as they thought they could then be secured, to a small people at a particular place and time. They were acutely conscious of the limits of their ability to secure these rights. When they were able to establish a "more perfect union" they understood full well how far from perfection they remained. It was all the new republic could do in the first century of its existence to keep the American experiment in freedom from failing miserably at home while other less fortunate experiments struggled to give birth to freedom in other parts of the world.

In the course of its history, the American people have many times fallen beneath the high standards they set for themselves at the beginning. They have strayed from those principles, and they have forgotten them, and become confused about them, and allowed misunderstood self-interest to obscure them. Our own experience has confirmed for us that democracy requires more of its citizens than any other form of government and that it is no accident that history provides so few examples of successful and enduring democracies. We count our blessings – the blessings of liberty – when we reflect with John Adams, "how few of the human race have ever had an opportunity of choosing a system of government for themselves and their children," and how few have chosen well.

The "genius" of the American people at the time of the American revolution and founding made it both possible and necessary to establish a country based on the republican principles proclaimed in the Declaration of Independence. As Jefferson said in explaining the genesis of the Declaration, the ideas expressed in it were "the common sense of the subject" in America. He was merely expressing "the American mind." It was only because the American people had learned to embrace republican principles that it was possible to establish an American republic. I mentioned in an earlier letter the American Founders' "honorable determination…to rest all our political experiments on the capacity of mankind for self-government." This was a determination, James Madison affirmed, "which animates every votary of freedom." But the Founders understood that any people that wished to be free, including the Americans, would have to demonstrate this capacity for themselves, and continue to demonstrate it each generation.

As the Declaration of Independence proclaimed, the just powers of government are derived from "the consent of the governed." Only a people prepared to consent to a free government are capable of establishing one; and once they have established it, as Ben Franklin never ceases to remind us, they will need to have what it takes to "keep it." At the least, this means a people must be prepared to recognize their own humanity and that of their fellow citizens; they will neither aspire to be masters nor submit to be slaves; they must be prepared to rule and be ruled in turn and to abide by the laws they claim the right to make for themselves.

We know from our own American case, even with all the natural and historical advantages we have had, that it is not easy to achieve or to keep and pass on these capacities for self-government. Experience and common sense tell us that these capacities are going to be even harder to achieve without the great advantages we have had. So let us be patient and moderate in our expectations from those who may face great disadvantages.

OHIO FARMER

No. 7

America and the World

April 5, 2011

To the Members of the 112th Congress:

America, on the President's orders, has intervened militarily in Libya; the President has given a speech explaining the intervention and the manner of it; the country and the world debate the matter as events unfold; the outcome remains uncertain. In his speech, the President insisted that, because the Libyan people faced "the prospect of violence on a horrific scale," America had a responsibility to act. "To brush aside...our responsibilities to our fellow human beings under such circumstances would have been a betrayal of who we are."

These letters are particularly concerned with "who we are" as a people and what this requires of our politics, domestic and foreign. So I leave aside for now the many other interesting and important questions swirling around the President's words and deeds, including his deference to the United Nations and his neglect of the United States Congress.

What does "who we are" tell us about how we should act toward the rest of the world? The President doesn't say much about what it is that makes us who we are, though he seems now to be affirming, on behalf of our fellow human beings, a kind of American exceptionalism, about which he had been studiously ambiguous in the past. We might begin to think about who we are by considering the two most important ideas in American political life. The first is found in the Declaration of Independence, which was cited in the last letter and will surely be cited often in future letters – the idea that "all men are created equal." The second is derived from this idea and is found in the opening phrase of the Constitution: it is the idea of consent expressed in the familiar words, "We the People of the United States." These are words and ideas, not to conjure with, but to consider carefully as events demand our attention and action at home and abroad. As long as Americans are Americans, these ideas will certainly continue to be essential ingredients of who we are. So what do they tell us about us?

The immediate practical purpose of the Declaration was to establish the right of the colonists to separate from the British Empire and its hereditary monarchy. In this case, declaring all men equal meant that God did not give one man or his family a divine right to rule other men. Human equality meant that government derived its powers justly only from "the consent of the governed." The claim that men were equal meant that not the accident of birth but the deliberate consent of men – "We the People" – was the only rightful basis for government.

The Declaration had a larger purpose, a broader reach, than the dispute between Great Britain and the United States of America. Its declaration of human equality denied not only a right to rule based on birth but a right to rule based on race or religion. Declaring all men equal meant that a common humanity was more fundamental than the accidents of race or religion that separated human beings.

The universality of this founding principle explains something of the claim the world has on American sympathies. Having based our national life on the equality of all men, we recognize that in principle any human being is a potential citizen of the United States. We feel an affinity with people around the world, especially those struggling for freedom or stricken by natural or manmade disasters. In our common humanity, we believe somehow that our hopes and fortunes are tied to theirs. These feelings can give rise to a sense of obligation that seems to be what President Obama has in mind – our "responsibilities to our fellow human beings," which he invokes when he says it would be a betrayal of who we are if we didn't intervene in the way he chose to do in Libya.

But in fact, of course, only Americans are American citizens. Our revolution began with a universal claim about human equality, but it culminated necessarily in the establishment of a particular nation. "We the People of the United States" are distinct from the other peoples of the world not by birth, race, or religion, but by the deliberate act of establishing ourselves as a different people. By this act of consent, the people of the United States committed themselves to each other, as distinct from all the others who live outside the bond of citizenship. In a world where freedom was scarce and tyranny commonplace (a world, in this respect, very like the one in which we continue to abide), we committed ourselves to establishing our own freedom and preserving the blessings of liberty in the United States, not to assisting the democratic aspirations of others or their recovery from disaster, however sympathetic we may be to the plight of our fellow men and however eager we may be to help them.

No model or mathematical formula can help us strike the proper balance between what we owe to our fellow men and what we owe to ourselves. Such balance is a matter for judgment and deliberation, as circumstances arise. This judgment will take into account the diverging claims of equality and consent, the former what Americans share with other peoples, the latter how we distinguished ourselves from them. These two American principles temper each other as we deliberate about how we as a people should act in a dangerous world of potential fellow citizens.

Our deliberations will be well served by reflecting that the American Founders thought the best thing Americans could do for the rest of the world was to succeed in our own experiment in freedom. As the Founders thought of it, the American cause – the cause of liberty – is the cause of mankind. If we could show by the success of our experiment that free government could be good government, this would be the greatest gift Americans could give to their fellow human beings – our own political well being would be a constant act of philanthropy. America's success would be cause for all men to rejoice. By the same token, failure of the American experiment in freedom would "deserve to be considered as the general misfortune of mankind."

From this point of view, Americans should want to know how our intervention in Libya enhances the prospects of the American experiment. If it does, the world will be a better place. If it doesn't, it betrays America's primary responsibility to our fellow human beings.

OHIO FARMER

No. 8

A Republican Form of Government
April 12, 2011

To the Members of the 112ᵗʰ Congress:

"The United States shall guarantee to every State in this Union a Republican Form of Government." So asserts the fourth section of Article IV of the Constitution.

The Supreme Court has had few occasions since 1789 to flesh out the meaning of that guarantee. It is clear that the Constitution prohibits any state or locality from regressing to feudalism – no Duchess of the Dakotas or Count of Mount Kisco will exercise political power over Americans. Beyond that, the Court said in 1849 that it was up to Congress, not the judiciary, to determine the criteria by which any state's government could be deemed insufficiently republican.

As is true of most questions before America's officials and citizens, *The Federalist Papers* are invaluable to comprehending this matter of republicanism. In *Federalist* 10, James Madison discusses the problem of faction, which he defines as "a number of citizens…united and actuated by some common impulse of passion, or of interest, adverse to the rights of other citizens, or to the permanent and aggregate interests of the community." The "latent causes of faction" are "sown in the nature of man," Madison warned, with the result that the "instability, injustice, and confusion introduced into the public councils, have, in truth, been the mortal diseases under which popular governments have everywhere perished."

Madison argued that *the* great danger was a faction comprising a majority of the electorate – whether united by a sectional, commercial, or religious interest – because it could operate democratically, winning a series of free and fair elections, even while disdaining the concerns and curtailing the rights of all citizens not belonging to that faction. He was more sanguine about a faction comprising a minority of the citizenry, because, he thought, the majority would be able to "defeat its sinister views by regular vote," rendering the faction "unable to execute and mask its violence under the forms of the Constitution."

Here Madison may have been too optimistic. The lessons of recent American politics suggest that minority factions can be more dangerous than he imagined. The modern phenomenon he failed to anticipate was a government entrusted with so many responsibilities, and so much power and money, that it becomes a faction unto itself, with its own passions and interests adverse to the rights of other citizens. Those in the control room have both the motive and means to steer the ship of state in directions advantageous to themselves, rather than ones preferred by the passengers who employ them.

The number and complexity of the issues being managed by government, at all levels, reach a point where the regular vote of the majority no longer prevails against the government faction. California, for example, boasts some 7,000 governmental entities – cities, counties, and "special purpose districts." Even the most responsible voters cannot possibly keep up with the daily changing minutiae being managed by these agencies. Americans who already have lives and jobs are not in a position to turn citizenship into a full time career. Among the respects in which all men are created equal is that everyone's week contains exactly 168 hours, regardless of how many public hearings your air quality management district schedules, or how many reports it makes available on its website.

Government employees, protected by strong unions and formidable civil service rules, have become an especially powerful and, in many cases, especially dangerous faction. In California, the power of those unions over one of the state's political parties is practically irresistible. And because they devote money and resources to low-turnout elections for school boards and transit districts, public employee unions have often been able to effect a travesty of collective bargaining – vigorous representation of their interests on both sides of the negotiating table. The recent debate about public sector unions in Wisconsin, led one chagrined citizen to reflect, "It's not democracy when citizens lose control over the pay and benefits of the people who work for them." Madison would agree.

Guaranteeing every state a republican form of government appears to be one of the Constitution's less difficult assignments. The harder part is to make sure that American government at every level is republican not just in form but in content. Are the people's elected representatives in charge of the government, or do life-tenured civil servants constitute a permanent government, one that can humor voters and legislators with token concessions, knowing it has all the expertise and time needed to out-maneuver and out-last intrusive voters and their representatives? That is the constitutional question of our age.

The fury and hysteria of the demonstrators opposed to the Wisconsin restrictions on public-employee unions inadvertently revealed the permanent government's assumption that mere politicians elected by mere voters had no moral authority to challenge the public employees' long-standing and cozy arrangements. The ongoing debates over public unions in Wisconsin, Ohio, and several other states are about fiscal solvency but they concern, even more fundamentally, the future of the republican form of government in America. We know from the relentless demonstrations in the streets of the Wisconsin city named after James Madison that the permanent government will go to great lengths to defend its prerogatives. Will the citizenry do what is necessary to reclaim *its* sovereign control over the *res publica* – the matters that properly belong to the public?

OHIO FARMER

No. 9

"The Kind of Country We Believe In"
April 19, 2011

To the Members of the 112th Congress:

On Wednesday last in his speech at George Washington University, President Obama observed that Americans are engaged in "one of the most important debates we can have." It is specifically a debate about "the size and role of government," but more generally, in the President's words, it is about "the kind of country that we believe in." He almost begins to sound like an Ohio Farmer! But seriously, it seems to me that the President is right about this and that it behooves us to take him and his words seriously – and to expect him to take himself seriously. This is not a time for sound bites and talking points, when words, as we all know is so often the case, are wielded as mere partisan weapons or are uttered to be forgotten.

The President tells us that he wants to "keep the dream of our founding alive" and "pass it on to our children." He invites Americans to be "patriotic," to have a "sense of responsibility – to each other and to our country." This all sounds pretty appealing – where is the debate? I think we find it in what the President means by this "sense of responsibility."

Americans, he says, have always "put faith in free markets and free enterprise"; "we are rugged individualists, a self-reliant people with a healthy skepticism of too much government." Amen. But, he adds immediately, America is also a country with federal programs "which guarantee us health care and a measure of basic income after a lifetime of hard work... [protect] us against unexpected job loss... [and provide] care for millions of seniors in nursing homes, poor children, [and] those with disabilities." America, he takes great trouble to emphasize, "would not be a great country without these commitments."

It is in these "commitments" that the President locates our "responsibility" as citizens. He would enlist our patriotism in upholding these commitments, without which he thinks America would not be great.

Here, to speak plainly, the President's "vision for America" (as he calls it) departs radically and self-consciously from the Founders' America and from all of American history until America was transformed by the New Deal and the Great Society beyond anything the Founders would recognize. In the President's vision, it is the New Deal and the Great Society that made America great, made it the kind of country he believes in.

All Americans are aware that decent medical care, good jobs, comfortable homes, and college educations are widely desired, and that countries are generally regarded as successful when, like America, they manage to make such desired things widely available. But all Americans also know that the Founders never supposed that the federal government should "guarantee" these and countless other social and economic goods as "rights" or "entitlements." It was the great triumph of the New Deal, extended by the Great Society, to establish these widely desired things as a new kind of rights – rights created by the state – as part of what Franklin Roosevelt called a "new constitutional order."

None of these New Deal or Great Society "rights" was obtained by actually amending the Constitution. They were assertions of what progressives think of as the "living constitution," that is a constitution that is subject to continual change as leaders with "vision" see where the path of Progress leads. In this progressive notion of a living constitution there is practically no limit to the "size and role of government."

So successful have the progressives been that hardly anyone in either party batted a law-abiding eye at the constitutionally shocking financial bailouts and rewriting of the bankruptcy law in just the past few years. The very idea of the rule of law disappears in the shadow of the living constitution. This is why supporters of the President's health care plan have reacted with stunned incredulity when asked where in the Constitution is the authority to enact such a plan. This is also why it is a substantial – though very incomplete – political victory just to raise that question. The great debate is between defenders of the Constitution and advocates of the living constitution, which renders the Constitution meaningless. The question of the size and role of government will be decided by the more fundamental debate.

Since the President raises the subject, is it really these New Deal commitments that make America great? Or would America enable itself to recover some of its greatness if it could free itself somewhat from the shackles of these commitments? These "commitments" teach an increasing number of Americans to wake every day looking to the federal government to take care of their basic needs and angrily resenting their country and their fellow citizens if they don't get what they want in a hurry. President Obama invites us to celebrate this dependency as our greatness. In his "vision," the more power we give the federal government – the more Americans are made dependent on the federal government – the greater we are as a people and a country. There is much willfulness in that vision. These progressive "rights" and "entitlements" teach Americans, very successfully, to think of themselves as organized interests – according to their jobs, race, gender, age, infirmities, and so on – interest groups clamoring incessantly for government to use its power over other citizens to better secure the "rights" of the interests. Is this a "sense of responsibility" that a great country could take pride in?

OHIO FARMER

No. 10

A Republic If We Can Keep It
April 26, 2011

To the Members of the 112th Congress:

That America is emphatically an "experiment" in self-government is a prominent theme of these letters. It is a noble experiment. We are honorably determined to stake the fate of our country on the capacity of Americans to govern themselves, knowing full well that this capacity is a rare and difficult thing for human beings to achieve and maintain. The capacity to govern ourselves is the capacity to set reasonable limits for ourselves. Our greatest act of self-government in this sense was the act by which "we, the people" submitted our sovereign power to the Constitution, which is at once our creation and the Supreme Law over us. We have seen in earlier letters various ways in which the progressive project – which produced the New Deal, the Great Society, and their contemporary successors – aims to replace the Constitution with a "living constitution," removing in principle all limits on what government might do or how it might do it. This has been the great challenge to self-government for the past century. It remains the great challenge for us. It has not been, and it will not be, easy to meet it.

In his speech on April 13 at George Washington University, President Obama explained in his own way why this is the case. "You see," he said, by way of explaining America's deficit problem, "most Americans tend to dislike government spending in the abstract, but like the stuff that it buys." Here, I think, the President is saying essentially what former Speaker of the House of Representatives, Thomas P. "Tip" O'Neill, meant by his most quoted maxim: "All politics is local." The progressive agenda counts on the fact that we Americans like the stuff government spending buys, just as Tip O'Neill counted on all politics being local.

Whenever it was that O'Neill uttered that nugget, he was speaking as a politician, not a political scientist. A Democrat who won his first election – to the Massachusetts legislature – in 1936, the year voters endorsed the

New Deal by overwhelmingly reelecting President Franklin Roosevelt, O'Neill won his last election – to a 17ᵗʰ term in Congress – in 1984, the year Ronald Reagan won *his* landslide reelection by challenging the propriety and feasibility of continuing the New Deal's commitment to activist government. In saying that all politics was local, O'Neill was pushing back against Reaganism, insisting that even if Americans had become dubious about activist government in general, they were still good New Dealers when it came to the particular benefits their own towns and neighborhoods could receive from government programs. Like Tip O'Neill, President Obama thinks – and not without reason – that Americans will be good New Dealers when push comes to shove. They will like the "stuff" they can get from government so much that, despite their self-governing inclinations, they will not be able to resist making themselves more and more dependent on government.

Reagan and O'Neill, the two antagonists of the 1980s, fought to a draw. Government spending on social programs grew more slowly under Reagan than under any other modern president, but he was never able to make good on the promise, announced in his first inaugural address, "to curb the size and influence of the Federal establishment." At the same time, the nation remained so wary of government's ambitions that two years after O'Neill's death a Democratic president, at the start of his own reelection campaign, found it necessary to declare, "The era of big government is over."

This political ambivalence, in which Americans have been constitutionalists in principle but progressives in practice (recognizing the dangers of unlimited government in the abstract, but liking "the stuff that it buys") has been durable, but there are signs it is becoming untenable. At the "local" level, the *New York Times* reported last year that many bond market experts "fear that as states struggle with their growing debts, investors could decide not to buy the debt of the weakest state or local governments," which "would force a crisis, since states cannot operate if they cannot borrow." The crisis seems most formidable in states like California, Illinois, New Jersey and New York – "blue" states, where big government remains very popular.

At the national level, we read of numbers that tend to numb the minds of even the most public-spirited citizens: the Congressional Budget Office recently forecast that the path charted in President Obama's 2012 budget would require the federal government to borrow $9.5 trillion over the next ten years. Federal government debt held by the public equaled 36% of the U.S. Gross Domestic Product in 2007, before the recession began, and 62% of GDP in 2010. By 2021 (just ten years from now), according to the CBO's scenario, it will equal 87% of GDP, $20.8 trillion, a level most economists believe would be debilitating, especially since the forces increasing federal deficits are likely to be even stronger in the third decade of this century than in the second. To cite just one problem, CBO projects interest payments on the national debt will rise from 1.7% of GDP in 2012 to 3.9% in 2021, by which time they will exceed $900 billion per year. That's just the interest, as the President reminded us.

It will not be easy for Americans to be constitutionalists in theory and progressives in practice if our elected government cannot pay its bills. If the lenders it depends on grow deeply skeptical about its ability to raise taxes or control spending, they will refuse to buy government bonds. (The manager of the world's largest bond fund recently reduced the percentage of its holdings in U.S. government-issued debt to zero.) Less drastically, lenders will demand a costly interest premium to offset the risk of default by state and local governments, or of inflation sponsored by a federal government to reduce its debt by devaluing the currency. At some point, the question becomes, not whether people like it when the government gives things to us and does things for us – as the President knows, both logic and experience demonstrate conclusively that we do – the crucial question becomes whether people like progressive government's endeavors enough to *pay for them*.

If we don't, if it becomes democratically impossible either to raise the taxes necessary to fund the government's operations, or to reduce the scope of its activities to a level that can be accommodated by the taxes the people *are* willing to pay, then the progressive project collapses. The people will no longer mediate the disparity between what they demand from government and what they surrender to it. Instead, decisive power over governance will pass to the lenders who keep public-sector operations afloat.

Such a result would be a financial debacle. The hard choices the people and their elected representatives now refuse to make will, in retrospect, be far easier than the policy changes an unsentimental bond market insists on as the price for further credit. But the political failure will be even more deplorable. In the well-known anecdote already recalled in these letters and sure to be noted again, Benjamin Franklin, upon being asked after the final meeting at Independence Hall in 1787 what kind of government the Constitutional Convention had fashioned, is supposed to have said, "A republic, if you can keep it." It is to America's credit that we have kept the republic, and in many ways strengthened and improved it, for 224 years. But we won't be able to keep it for many more years if we do not return to our self governing ways.

OHIO FARMER

No. 11

The Course of Human Events
May 3, 2011

To the Members of the 112th Congress:

How endlessly interesting and full of surprises is the course of human events. For the past two weeks, in hundreds of Congressional districts throughout the 50 states, we citizens witnessed lawmakers of both parties, on recess, engaging their constituents in conversations about the nation's business in town hall meetings and other forums. The President was hosting his own town hall meetings, from Virginia to Facebook headquarters in California, and conducting interviews with local television stations in cities across the country. The central issue was the budget of the United States Government for the fiscal year 2012, and the conversation was shaped primarily by two competing proposals for that budget, the one put forward by President Obama on February 14, the other put forward in early April by the House Budget Committee chaired by Representative Paul Ryan (R-WI) and approved by the House on April 15. In light of the country's debt and deficit crises, barring surprises in the course of human events, this looked likely to be the big issue of the coming months, leading up to the 2012 elections.

The issue is urgent and complicated (to say the least!) and the conversations were lively. For the most part, they seemed like a healthy spectacle of James Madison's extended republic at work: a wide variety of contending interests and opinions jostling with one another in a robust American way, from which one might reasonably hope that eventually the "cool and deliberate sense" of the community would make some progress toward the public good. Certainly – you not being angels, and this being free, democratic politics – one could witness displays among the lawmakers of what Publius called "talents for low intrigue and the little arts of popularity." I needn't name names here, and can put it down to an excess of zeal to please us, the people. And as for us citizens, in more than one instance, unfortunately, some of us became so animated that we had to be removed from the premises by the police. In fairness to the parties involved in these cases, those who had to be removed seemed to be on one side of the issue. But similar behavior, certainly, could be attributed to those on the other side on other occasions. We are, after all, "the people," and no more angelic than our elected representatives, and sometimes our democratic behavior does not reflect very well on our human nature.

One of the hopes of these letters is to connect our contemporary political conversation with the tradition of American political discourse that has enriched our politics for over two centuries. In this instance, it may be helpful to observe that, by our less than angelic behavior, we merely confirm Publius's observation, that in "cases of great national discussion" we should not be surprised if a "torrent of angry and malignant passions will be let loose," or that the opposing parties "mutually hope to evince the justness of their opinions, and to increase the number of their converts by the loudness of their declamations and the bitterness of their invectives."

Maybe our political passions will be calmed somewhat by the wise and beautiful lessons of moderation offered by Alexander Hamilton (a man himself perhaps not always moderate) in *Federalist* 1:

> So numerous indeed and so powerful are the causes which serve to give a false bias to the judgment, that we, upon many occasions, see wise and good men on the wrong as well as on the right side of questions of the first magnitude to society. This circumstance, if duly attended to, would furnish a lesson of moderation to those who are ever so much persuaded of their being in the right in any controversy. And a further reason for caution, in this respect, might be drawn from the reflection that we are not always sure that those who advocate the truth are influenced by purer principles than their antagonists.

James Madison adds his own moderating wisdom in *Federalist* 37:

> It is a misfortune, inseparable from human affairs, that public measures are rarely investigated with that spirit of moderation which is essential to a just estimate of their real tendency to advance or obstruct the public good;

and that this spirit is more apt to be diminished than promoted, by those occasions which require an unusual exercise of it.

Our civic moderation might be further strengthened by the reminder we received on Sunday night that, whatever the lively differences among ourselves in our pursuit of happiness, we are at war – and have been ever since that surprising turn in the course of human events on September 11, 2001. Whatever our differences, we join past generations of Americans, going back to the Revolutionary generation, in mutually pledging to one another "our lives, our fortunes, and our sacred honor." The sacrifices of many patriots teach us constantly that this is no vagrant commitment, that there is some enduring thing in our country for the sake of which Americans make such a pledge, generation after generation, each to all and all to each. They teach us to summon the better angels of our nature to our national conversations as we pursue our happiness in freedom.

A young Abraham Lincoln instructed a group of high school students over 170 years ago that "[w]e find ourselves under the government of a system of political institutions, conducing more essentially to the ends of civil and religious liberty, than any of which the history of former times tells us." Like Lincoln, our generation of Americans inherited these blessings of liberty. There is no greater earthly bequest we can have received. It is our greatest duty and our highest honor as Americans to pass on this inheritance unimpaired – indeed, strengthened and improved in every way possible, to our children. This seems to me to be what our great national conversation is about. Let's rise to the seriousness of the question.

OHIO FARMER

No. 12

Our Justice
May 10, 2011

To the Members of the 112th Congress:

The attackers would come out of the forest, sweeping across a settlement or isolated homestead, killing and burning as they went. Depending on their strength, the attackers might move far into settled territory or simply withdraw after the destruction of one settler family. But sooner or later they would disappear into the wilderness from which they had come.

The settlers fortified their homes and formed militias to defend themselves. But the attackers struck without warning and, if they withdrew quickly, could avoid the organized defense of the settlers. It became necessary, then, to attack the attackers. They seldom stood and fought in the European way. They preferred ambush and skirmish, so the settlers fought this way too. They also attacked their enemy's settlements, destroying crops and inhabitants, old and young, male and female. Sometimes the enemy could be found not too far away. Other times it was necessary to track them deep into the wilderness.

This was a brutal business, not the almost gentlemanly endeavor that organized eighteenth-century warfare aspired to. Its necessity did not disguise its brutality or even excuse all instances of it.

This kind of fighting began shortly after the founding of the first settlements and continued episodically for 100 years or so after the founding of the nation. That such fighting was part of the American experience and has become part of it again can tell us something about "who we are," a phrase President Obama has used more than once when discussing the killing of bin Laden.

First, those in frontier settlements open to attack had an immediate experience of perhaps the most basic account we offer of ourselves. We join together for our common defense and common good, since no individual or single family is alone sufficient to achieve such ends. The frontier militia consisting of all able-bodied men was a direct expression of this idea, embodying in a more effective form the right of every individual to self-defense. More broadly, we hold, all legitimate government rests on the same idea. The government has only the authority that we give it.

Much has changed in the more than 200 years since the founding of the United States, but this elemental idea about the relationship of citizens to their government has not changed. Those who killed bin Laden carried weapons but were armed above all with the authority of the people of the United States. That is what dignified their violence and distinguished it from the brutality authored by their target.

The killing of bin Laden was not only authorized; it was also just. It may turn out that bin Laden was still involved in active plotting against the United States. If so, his killing was an act of self-defense, no less necessary and just than the raids Americans carried out against their enemies in the forested wilderness long ago.

But whether or not bin Laden was plotting against us, his death was still just. It was an act of revenge; and revenge, giving someone what he deserves, is a form of justice. We may hope that bin Laden's death will discourage others from continuing his work, but that was not the point of killing bin Laden. Revenge, even more than self-defense, is an assertion of self-worth. Its principal audience is not those on whom vengeance falls, but those in whose name vengeance is carried out. It is their statement above all to themselves that they are not the sort to be affronted or assaulted. "The world is what it is," the poet has written, "and those who are nothing or allow themselves to become nothing have no place in it." Those who take revenge testify that they are something rather than nothing. The more dogged and unrelenting the pursuit in the wilderness, the more spectacular its culmination, the greater is the testimony of who they are.

The good of revenge requires something more elemental still. Taking revenge takes courage. It took courage to authorize the attack. It took courage to carry it out. Courage is perhaps the most elemental virtue but without it, there can be no others. It is what holds an individual as well as a nation together in the face of life's dangers. Done in our name, with our authority, the killing of bin Laden should encourage us for the dangers we yet face.

OHIO FARMER

No. 13

A Decent Respect

May 17, 2011

To the Members of the 112th Congress:

Following the killing of Osama bin Laden on the orders of the President of the United States, some prominent European politicians, clerics, and journalists condemned the act. Americans, many of whom continue publicly to applaud bin Laden's death, were likened to "Muslims celebrating in the Gaza Strip" following the attacks on America on September 11, 2001. What should Americans think of such criticisms? How, more generally, should we regard the opinions of the peoples and governments of other nations?

To take the second question first, the natural American place to begin a response seems to be with the Declaration that announced our independence to the world in 1776, a declaration that was offered out of "a decent respect to the opinions of mankind," which "requires that [Americans] should declare the causes which impel them to the separation [from Great Britain]." Declaring the causes of our actions – giving reasons for them – was an act of respect for the opinions of mankind because it treated mankind as if their opinions could respond to reasons. This was a hopeful view of the human condition. It did honor to human nature and imposed expectations on human capacities.

The central idea proclaimed in the declaration – the main reason for our action – was the self-evident truth that "all men are created equal," that is, that all men everywhere and at all times possess by nature equal rights to life, liberty, and the pursuit of happiness. Of course, this was an idea that seemed self-evidently untrue to the hereditary monarchs and nobility of Europe. So America showed its first respect for the opinions of mankind by disagreeing with most of them! – and in the same breath telling the peoples of the world how they might show greater respect for themselves, by recognizing and asserting the rights of their own humanity.

Americans were keenly aware how difficult it would be to live up to the principle they were proclaiming – how heroic and continuous an effort would be required of themselves or any people that aspired to rise to equality. This very difficulty is partly what makes it such an "honorable determination…to rest all our political experiments on the capacity of mankind for self-government." As I have written in an earlier letter, "Any people that wished to be free, including the Americans, would have to demonstrate this capacity for themselves, and continue to demonstrate it each generation." What could be more honorable to human nature? What could show greater respect to mankind and their opinions?

The American experiment claims to be a glorious experiment because it aims, for the first time in human history, to make actual the potential for self-government that we Americans insist human beings have by nature. This is what the Founders meant when they soberly – and by no means arrogantly – reflected on the fact that it seems to have been reserved to "the people of this country, by their conduct and example, to decide the important question, whether societies of men are really capable or not of establishing good government from reflection and choice."

The greatest respect Americans can show for the opinions of mankind is to take responsibility for being the kind of self-governing people we invite all people to be. Taking such responsibility may require, in the sometimes hard course of human events, the killing of the bin Ladens of this world. As I said in my last letter, our men who killed bin Laden were "armed above all with the authority of the people of the United States. That is what dignified their violence and distinguished it from the brutality authored by their target." How can the "authority of the people" – us – dignify such an act, raise it above the barbarism and savagery of bin Laden and all who support him and cheer him on? Only, I think, if "we the people" are the people we claimed to be, insisted on being, at our beginning – a people claiming the right to govern ourselves, as we proclaim and respect the same right for all other human beings; a people doing everything in our power to cultivate in ourselves the capacities necessary to vindicate this natural human right.

Such a people will conduct themselves so that an attack upon them could never in truth be said to be a blessing to mankind; so that if they are compelled to some harsh measure like the killing of bin Laden, the world may truly be said to be better off because of it. Such a people will arrange the political affairs of their land so that no one could with justice wish for the displacement of their rule by that of an enemy. They will be neither self-aggrandizing nor self-sacrificing. They will approach the world, in Washington's words, as their "interest, guided by justice, shall counsel."

Such a people will understand that politics, though it must sometimes resort to harsh necessities like the killing of bin Ladens, is in the final analysis not reducible to such necessities. Even Sun Tzu, that great teacher of the art of war, understood that "[t]hose who excel in war [must] first cultivate their own humanity and justice," that war is conducted ultimately for the sake of peace. Closer to home, our own John Adams offered his American version of that human wisdom, when he reflected, "I must study Politicks and War that my sons may have liberty to study Mathematicks and Philosophy." The successful practice of the arts of necessity – which are forced upon us by the needs of mere life – seems to be a necessary condition for the flourishing of the arts of freedom – which we pursue because they prepare us to deserve, by using well, "the blessings of liberty."

What about the more particular question, about American rejoicings at the killing of bin Laden? Of course, no self-respecting, self-governing people will condone dancing in the street to celebrate cruel necessities. Nor would it be a proud moment for such a people to make these cruel necessities applause lines in campaign rallies. But only a good people – a people able to take responsibility for choosing right over wrong – can be a self-governing people, and the world will be a sad place when good people can no longer rejoice at the triumph, however small and incomplete, of good over evil.

OHIO FARMER

No. 14

The Commerce Clause
May 24, 2011

To the Members of the 112th Congress:

Are there any limits, in principle, remaining on federal power in America? We have seen in these letters that there are elected and appointed officials and citizens in the country who would answer, for all practical purposes: "No." We have also seen that the question is not closed and that it is not just for lawyers or judges to decide; it belongs to all the people, and to all three branches of government. Let us reflect on one path our nation took that, over the course of a couple of generations, made assertions of unlimited federal power commonplace in America; and let us consider some recent decisions by the courts that remind us that the constitutional conversation is not over.

Much of the current debate over federal authority (including the lawsuit over the Patient Protection and Affordable Care Act – PPACA or Obamacare) turns on how much power Congress has under the Commerce Clause, which states that "Congress shall have Power to…regulate Commerce…among the several States." The Founders inserted the Commerce Clause into the Constitution to correct a deficiency in the Articles of Confederation, which led states to impose duties on goods from other states, or goods which traveled through their states. James Madison lamented that, in some cases, it was cheaper to buy goods from Great Britain than from a neighboring state given the taxes and duties that the states were placing on the goods. The Commerce Clause was intended to give Congress the authority to facilitate the free flow of goods among the states.

In the late 19th and early 20th century, states began to regulate areas like working conditions, hours, and crop production and pricing, but progressives argued that federal regulation was necessary to bring about more reforms. Many of these policies enjoyed (and continue to enjoy) some measure of popular support. But there was a problem for those who wished to implement the policies at the federal level: the Constitution provided no general authority to regulate businesses. And so, progressives and New Dealers in Congress and the White House turned to the Commerce Clause.

For a time, progressives and New Dealers were politically successful in promoting their agenda in Congress and the White House, but they had less success in the courts, which found that, while Congress had authority to regulate some local activities that affected interstate commerce, the authority was limited. With retirements, replacements, and threats of court packing, the Court's position changed over time. By 1942, the Court decided a case in a way that many believed spelled the end of any limitation on federal authority. In *Wickard v. Filburn*, the Court found that the federal government could regulate wheat grown by a farmer for personal consumption under the theory that such local activity, when aggregated, could substantially affect interstate commerce.

After *Wickard*, Congress passed innumerable regulations covering business and non-business activity alike based upon the Commerce Clause and the theory that, when aggregated, just about any activity could substantially affect commerce. Over the course of decades, presidents of both parties signed legislation based upon expanding notions of federal authority, and on the popularity of the underlying legislative policy, and the courts acceded to the enterprise. But the constitutional conversation continued. In the mid-1990s, the Supreme Court struck down the Gun Free School Zones Act, finding that the federal government does not have a general police power to regulate the non-economic act of carrying a gun in a school zone. Next, the Court struck down a provision of the Violence Against Women Act (VAWA), which permitted individuals to sue their alleged attackers for gender-motivated violence. The Court again found that non-economic violent actions could not be aggregated to establish a substantial connection to interstate commerce.

Both of these bills were popular, passing Congress with overwhelming majorities. And why not? Very few would argue in the abstract against banning guns at schools or prohibiting gender-motivated violence. Given the popularity of the legislation, the Court's decisions were first widely attacked, but over time they began to receive acceptance in quarters where few expected it. A constitutional conversation was kindled, between the branches – and among the people. Some feminists, for example, who chastised the Court for striking down VAWA, recognized that they did not like the idea of a federal government with unrestricted regulatory authority over their lives. Citizens and their representatives began to talk not merely about whether the policy objectives sought by Congress were desirable, but whether the federal government was empowered to act in that sphere at all.

Which brings us back to Obamacare. Is it bad policy? That is a very important question. But whatever we might think about that, let us not fail to give our full and best attention to the separate and even more important question: Is it constitutional? Even the courts that have upheld the act have recognized that there is something unprecedented at play. Never before has Congress ordered citizens to buy something, and penalized them for failing to do so. If this is permitted, what are the limits? Congress doesn't have the power to pass any law it wants; it has the powers given to it by the American people through our Constitution – nothing less, but also nothing more. Limits matter. A law based on the assumption that the commerce power is unlimited violates the basic principle of constitutional self-government.

What limits are there to federal authority? This should be the focus of our constitutional conversation.

OHIO FARMER

No. 15

The Spirit of Checks and Balances
May 31, 2011

To the Members of the 112th Congress:

Senator Harry Reid of Nevada recently stated that the National Labor Relations Board (NLRB), the regulatory agency established by the 1935 National Labor Relations Act, was "created in the same spirit of checks and balances" as the U.S. Constitution itself. NLRB "acts as a check on employers and employees alike," said Reid. "It safeguards employees' rights to unionize or not to unionize, if they so choose, it mediates allegations of unfair labor practices, and it does all this independent of any outside influence."

Reid was defending NLRB's decision to issue a complaint against Boeing, the aircraft manufacturer, for opening a new production facility in South Carolina to produce its latest commercial aircraft, the 787 "Dreamliner." The NLRB filed its complaint, which is similar to an indictment in criminal court, because its acting general counsel contends that the company decided to open the South Carolina plant in order to threaten the International Association of Machinists (IAM), the union representing workers at Boeing's 787 plant in Seattle, Washington.

The reasoning is that Boeing was attempting to punish IAM for going out on strike in the past, and intimidate it from going out on strike in the future, by opening a new facility to produce the 787 in a state where only 2.8% of private-sector employees are union members. Such an action, the complaint alleges, unlawfully discriminates against those Seattle workers represented by the union. Demonstrating a nice gift for irony, NLRB insists that it does not seek to prohibit Boeing from running its South Carolina factory, only to prevent the company from illegally intimidating IAM. The NLRB remedy, however, is to require Boeing to open and operate a second, unionized 787 factory in Seattle – one that would, of course, turn the non-unionized plant in South Carolina into a hugely expensive redundancy.

Reid's argument could be considered a faint, though distorted, echo of the assertion in *Federalist* 51 that the Constitution's "policy of supplying, by opposite and rival interests, the defect of better motives, might be traced through the whole system of human affairs, private as well as public." In classical economic thought, of course, the defect of better motives in private affairs is supplied when individuals seeking their own benefit wind up inadvertently improving the lives of others by offering goods and services that are of higher quality or sold at lower prices than those provided by their competitors. As Adam Smith wrote in *The Wealth of Nations*, "It is not from the benevolence of the butcher, the brewer, or the baker, that we expect our dinner, but from their regard to their own interest. We address ourselves, not to their humanity but to their self-love, and never talk to them of our necessities but of their advantages."

When he suggests that it is a logical extension of the American founding to have a government agency tell a company where it may and must locate its factories and offices, Reid is reflecting the New Deal idea that market competition was no longer a sufficient restraint on powerful industrial enterprises. The economist John Kenneth Galbraith argued for the same view in *American Capitalism*: regulatory agencies and labor unions imparted to our economic system the benefits of "countervailing power." Such entities would offset the dominance of giant corporations in markets that were, Galbraith argued, theoretically but not effectively free.

Galbraith and Reid notwithstanding, for a federal agency to lay the groundwork to order a private company to build its products here and not there is contrary to, not consistent with, the logic of the American founding. For one thing, the Constitution protects both the ability of the individual states to govern their internal affairs, and the free flow of commerce between the states. States are prohibited, for example, from levying duties on goods "imported" from other states of the Union. The Constitution was, in this sense, the original North American Free Trade Agreement.

When Congress amended the National Labor Relations Act in 1947, it explicitly authorized state governments to enact "right-to-work" laws, which stipulate that private employers may not fire employees who refuse to join a union or pay union dues. Since a labor union is a kind of cartel, where sellers of labor agree not to compete against one another, right-to-work laws have generally had the intended effect of preventing unions from forming and growing. Since 1947, 22 states, including South Carolina but not Washington, have enacted such laws.

Since right-to-work provisions are legal, and the free flow of commerce between states is constitutional, it's hard to see how the NLRB's proposed course of action can be wise. If the agency winds up forcing Boeing to build production facilities in Washington, when the company would rather build them in South Carolina, it will nullify Boeing's right to choose how to run its business, and South Carolina's right to choose how to run its state.

There are other problems with Reid's position. Although the Constitution states, "All legislative powers herein granted shall be vested in a Congress of the United States," Reid means to restrain Congress when he describes NLRB, an entity created by Congress, as an agency that does its work "independent of any outside influence." The outside influence he resents is Congress itself, or at least its Republican members. For Republicans in Congress to object to NLRB's course of action concerning Boeing is "inappropriate ... disgraceful and dangerous."

Reid does not, apparently, have a gift for irony. He is outraged that elected members of Congress are objecting to an NLRB inspector bringing a complaint about the violation of NLRB rules before an NLRB administrative law judge – because of the threat such political "interference" poses to the "spirit of checks and balances." The genius of the Constitution was to separate legislative, executive, and judicial powers. The genius of the New Deal was to combine them in agencies whose employees and friends want to keep them independent from – politics. Independent, that is, of democratic self-government. Independent, in other words, from the people.

"Which Side Are You On?" asks the anthem of the American labor movement. We know which side Harry Reid is on, and it isn't James Madison's.

OHIO FARMER

No. 16

The Lost Art of Legislation
June 7, 2011

To the Members of the 112th Congress:

One of the head-scratching moments of the congressional debate leading up to the passage last year of the Patient Protection and Affordable Care Act (otherwise known as "Obamacare") was then-House Speaker Nancy Pelosi's response when asked about the contents of the 2,000-page draft law [see Ohio Farmer Letter, "Reconstitutionalizing America"]. You recall that Speaker Pelosi said, "We have to pass the bill so you can see what's in it." She was not alone with this thought. Senator Max Baucus, chairman of the Senate Finance Committee that had key jurisdiction over the health care bill, said something similar: "I don't think you want me to waste my time to read every page of the health care bill. You know why? It's statutory language. We hire experts."

Both comments generated considerable ridicule, especially from people who opposed the legislation. But both comments bring to light a fundamental fact of modern American government: Congress no longer "legislates" (that is, passes binding universal laws) in the way the Founders intended when they wrote the Constitution. Instead, Congress passes general statutes containing policy goals, but delegates the power to write the actual operating laws to executive branch administrators and independent agencies. In practical terms, this means that the executive branch and independent administrative agencies, rather than Congress, actually determine the details – the real law as it will operate on citizens. This might be acceptable except that the process of administrative government is increasingly arbitrary, and arbitrary government is the very definition of lawlessness.

Some short sections of the health care law will require hundreds of pages of detailed regulations, which administrative experts are going to spend the next several years working out. Sen. Baucus is right: the statutory language does not tell you how the law will operate in practice.

The 2,000 page statute will grow to perhaps 30,000 pages by the time the administrative agencies finish filling in the blanks. Here is another wrinkle: the health care law shows that Congress is now passing "laws" that cannot take effect as written, because they are so woefully incomplete.

Two recent news items highlight this problem. First, the health care law contains a number of mandates on insurance companies and businesses intended to correct what are widely regarded as abuses of the private marketplace for insurance and health services. Yet the Department of Health and Human Services is handing out "waivers" – exemptions from the letter of the law – like Halloween candy to labor unions, big businesses (McDonald's), small businesses (boutique restaurants in San Francisco), and several of the large insurance companies who are thought to be part of the problem. The health care law's waiver process is like telling the traffic police that they get to set a "safe" speed limit, but then allowing them to decide that different motorists get to drive at different speeds. We're no longer equal under the law when a government administrator can decide who has to obey a law and who doesn't. Prior to this moment, federal government waivers tended to be applied only to state and local governments in their implementation of federally-funded programs like welfare or highway construction or public education. Now the government is extending waivers to private citizens and their businesses, treating equal people unequally.

The second news item ringing alarm bells is the decision of the National Labor Relations Board (NLRB) ordering the Boeing aircraft company to build its new Dreamliner airplane in Washington state, rather than South Carolina, where Boeing has already spent over $1 billion building a new assembly line for the Dreamliner [see Ohio Farmer Letter, "The Spirit of Checks and Balances"]. The NLRB based its decision on a clause in the Wagner Act that says private companies may not "retaliate" against labor unions, and argues that locating aircraft production in a non-union state amounts to "retaliation" against the unions that have struck Boeing three times in the last decade in Washington state. The "retaliation" clause has never been interpreted this way before; and, in any case, we should be asking why an independent agency – the NLRB – gets to enforce the law, rather than the Justice Department, an executive department politically accountable to the President, working through the ordinary federal court system. The NLRB was set up to provide labor unions a privileged position in our legal order, but it means that any company might be prohibited from moving or expanding from a unionized state to a right-to-work state. It is doubtful Congress meant the statute to be construed this way when it was passed, or that any Congress would consent to such a construction. As a practical matter the Boeing case is likely to be isolated, but that just makes the Boeing precedent all the more troubling, as it reveals our labor law to be arbitrary. And the NLRB is hardly alone in this style of unaccountable government that blurs the separation of powers between the branches. The Environmental Protection Agency operates in a similar fashion, and the new financial regulations of the Dodd-Frank law passed in response to the banking crisis of 2008 will also be determined by the administrative organs of government.

It may be necessary for Congress to delegate the working out of many details to administrative agencies. But this practice has come with the high cost of degrading the deliberative function of Congress's lawmaking power. The easy delegation of the details is why many large laws are rushed to passage in a less than transparent manner. True debate and deliberation has atrophied. This slow abdication of legislative responsibility on the part of Congress started many decades ago, and is no simple matter to fix. As a general principle members of Congress ought to refuse to vote for statutes that delegate large amounts of the real lawmaking to another branch. If the health care law's perverse consequences (such as the possibility that, without a waiver, McDonald's would have had to drop health insurance for all its employees) were laid at the feet of Congress, then Congress would write laws more carefully, or move more quickly to amend them as they should. In one word, is this not a good occasion for Congress to assume more *responsibility* for its actions?

OHIO FARMER

No. 17

Political Success and Governmental Failure
June 14, 2011

To the Members of the 112th Congress:

In his first debate with Stephen Douglas in 1858, Abraham Lincoln said, "In this and like communities, public sentiment is everything. With public sentiment, nothing can fail; without it nothing can succeed."

Seven score and 13 years after those debates we are now engaged in a great political contest over whether the welfare state established by the New Deal and built up continuously since 1932 can long endure. Its growth over the past eight decades and the financial crisis confronting it today suggest the need to qualify Lincoln's rule: Public sentiment may ensure political success for a policy, but it does not rule out governmental failure. Indeed, a policy can be a governmental failure precisely because it is a political success.

It is our pride as Americans that our government must answer to our consent. If we insist on consenting to bad government, it will be very hard for a democratic government to be good. When Lincoln was speaking of public sentiment, he knew that it was a public he had to persuade to do the right thing, a public with many strong inclinations to do the wrong thing. His point was that this is the most important job a politician has in a democracy – to persuade the people to do the right thing.

In a *New York Times* public opinion poll last year, 76 percent of all respondents agreed that "the benefits from government programs such as Social Security and Medicare [are] worth the costs of those programs." Even 62 percent of those who said they support the "tea party" movement thought so! It's hardly a surprise that public sentiment supports these programs, the mainstays of our welfare state.

The governmental problem is that the benefits of these programs are not only worth what they cost, but worth far more than they cost. According to a recent study, a husband and wife, each born in 1915 and each earning the average wage during their working years, would have retired in 1980 having paid a total of $190,000 in Social Security taxes and $15,600 in Medicare taxes. That couple could expect to receive, on average, $446,000 in Social Security benefits and $132,000 in Medicare benefits. Depending on health and longevity, some couples received more and some less but the average benefits from the two programs would have totaled $578,000.

We shouldn't be surprised that government programs become highly popular when, in effect, they hand out $372,400 checks rather than gold watches to new retirees. Being popular isn't the same as being sustainable, however, and the popularity of Social Security and Medicare has gone a long way to help them become unsustainable. The New Deal's architects and advocates believed that rapid economic and population growth would make it possible to perpetuate social insurance programs' large windfalls. There's no prospect, however, for the economic growth that would allow the federal government to pay out in the first half of the 21st century the kind of social insurance benefits that Americans came to expect in the second half of the 20th. And as to population, everyone knows that people these days are having fewer children or, in many more cases now than in the past, none at all. As a result, we see the formation of a demographic bulge, with a disproportionately large number of older people receiving benefits from social insurance programs and a disproportionately small number of younger people paying taxes to finance those benefits.

We have no choice, then, but to address the financial imbalances built into our welfare state. The Democratic Party, defined since 1932 by championing the cause of an ever-larger welfare state, wants government spending to be the independent variable that determines tax levels. The Republican Party, home to New Deal opponents in the 1930s and New Deal skeptics ever since, wants government spending to be the dependent variable determined by taxes. Democrats hope that when push comes to shove, and we can no longer borrow our way out of the welfare state's rickety financing, the people will come to the conclusion that large reductions in welfare state benefits are unthinkable, and they will support the large, widely applied tax increases that will certainly be needed to continue and expand our social insurance programs. Republicans have the opposite hope – that when voters come to realize the size of the tax increases needed to sustain our welfare state they will, at long last, be amenable to the kind of big reductions in government spending that have been ballot box losers for nearly a century.

America's welfare state has grown for the past 80 years because people like its benefits. There are two reasons it hasn't grown even faster. The lesser one is that people had some qualms, now largely forgotten, about the legitimacy of having the government redistribute wealth from some people to others. The more politically consequential reason is that people like getting what the welfare state provides much more than they like paying for what it costs.

The Democratic Party has worked hard for many years to reassure people that generous welfare state benefits really are compatible with modest taxes, or ones that only very rich people and large corporations will have to worry about. There are two problems with this reassurance. First, it's not true: a welfare state like the comprehensive ones in most European countries requires the kind of heavy, widely applied taxes common in Europe. Second, the fact that Democrats have always gravitated to the far-fetched argument that we can have New York's social welfare system and South Dakota's taxes suggests they're afraid that most Americans won't vote for the comprehensive welfare state Democrats advocate if the price is shown in big print on the first page, rather than buried in a footnote. Those fears form the foundation of the Republicans' hopes that the welfare state we'll end up with – if its costs are honestly reckoned and realistically shared – will be much smaller (and much smarter) than the one we have now.

We Americans celebrate our capacity to govern ourselves. Here certainly is a test of our capacity. The government can't solve this problem without the help of the people, because the right government can't get elected unless we the people are wise enough to elect those who are committed to make the choices that are necessary. Are we? Can we be persuaded to be?

OHIO FARMER

No. 18

"American Leadership"?
June 21, 2011

To the Members of the 112th Congress:

Does America have a unique right and duty to lead the rest of the world? Many decent, patriotic citizens, with no wish to be boastful or presumptuous, and without probing the question too hard, might be inclined in some general way to answer in the affirmative. And if these citizens have been heeding the pronouncements of their elected and appointed representatives recently, they may be forgiven for getting the impression that their affirmative should be emphatic.

"The world is counting on us," Secretary of State Clinton said a few months ago. "The United States can, must and will lead in the new century." Secretary of Defense Gates made a similar point when talking about the defense budget, reiterating his "fundamental belief" that "America does have a special position and set of responsibilities on this planet." Congressman Paul Ryan echoed the sentiment in a recent speech about the effects of America's deficit and debt on our place in the world. "We must lead," he said, "and a central element of maintaining American leadership is the promotion of our moral principles."

One advantage the American Founders hoped for from a large and diverse representative republic was that our elected and appointed representatives might "refine and enlarge the public views" when they chose to honor a subject with their attention. But we all know that there is a relentless demand for public officials to make public pronouncements, and it is not surprising when under such pressure their pronouncements do not always display the wisdom or even the good sense we might hope for. Still, these letters optimistically take the speech of our public officials seriously, in the determined hope that they too will take it seriously and not wantonly strew sound bites around in the word-cluttered world. So when, in the interest of the public views, we take seriously the sentiments quoted above, we can't help wondering whether they could use a little more refining and enlarging.

If we follow the logic of the argument, and we are not sure we do, America is to be understood to have this right and responsibility to lead because of some combination of its power and its principles, and it would appear that its power in some way and some degree flows from its principles. The happy reflection occurs to us that America's principles are more broadly shared today than when they were declared over two and a quarter centuries ago to the world of hereditary monarchs and aristocracies of Europe. Regimes of political and economic freedom like America's have become the practice in many places around the world. If our principles confer a right to lead, then wouldn't many other nations have that right as well?

But, it might be said, these other nations do not have our power. It is our power, then, that uniquely qualifies us to lead. Does this not come uncomfortably close to the distasteful claim that might makes right? What could be further from our principles? This is a claim for bullies and tyrants, not for a free people.

Our power and principles cannot be separated, it might be argued. We are most powerful when we are most principled, and the unique combination of our power and principles makes us uniquely fit to lead. There is surely something appealing – and true! – in the idea that "right makes might." When Americans appealed in 1776 "to the supreme judge of the world for the rectitude of our intentions," we were acknowledging that our justice would be an ally in our struggle for independence and in all else we could hope to do as a nation. But everyone knows that adherence to principle can also be costly, that it can and often does, therefore, decrease one's power and may even take one's life. Adherence to principle despite the cost is noble, but nobility is not the same as power. We are most noble, perhaps, but not necessarily most powerful, when we are most principled.

There is another way in which adherence to our principles makes us less powerful, at least relatively. The most fundamental principle of our politics is the idea of human equality. From this principle we derive our commitment to human freedom. Human freedom, political and economic, leads in turn to greater wealth and, to the extent that wealth is power, to greater power. As our principles become more widely shared around the world – our constant hope – others will become more wealthy and powerful, too. So, the more widely our principles spread, the more our power will decline relative to others, diminishing our capacity to lead.

The notion that America has a unique right and responsibility to lead the rest of the world thus seems in various ways to be factually problematic; seems to tend toward the unwelcome view that might makes right; and seems at best confused or disheartening about the relationship between power and principle. One cannot help thinking that, under the constant and almost irresistible pressure to say *something,* our nation's spokesmen have spoken on this subject more from reflex than reflection. It is always regrettable when those who should be refining the public views muddy the waters a bit instead. But the reflex was understandable, arising as it seems to do from an idea, if a confused idea, of an age old American theme – the theme of American exceptionalism, which we will take up in earnest in our next letter.

OHIO FARMER

No. 19

A City Upon a Hill
June 28, 2011

To the Members of the 112th Congress:

Is America exceptional? Is it unique among the nations? If so, what makes it so? And what are the implications of the fact? These are not policy questions, but questions about ideas and historical circumstances that are at the foundation of policies. They are the kinds of questions, it seems, that you and other elected and appointed public officials are often compelled for no particularly good reason to answer, as was the President a short time ago. Perhaps this may sometimes seem a tedious requirement of your job, especially when journalists asking the questions have no interest other than ginning up a headline. And so it is understandable if on occasion you reach for plausible sounding formulas in the hope that they will not cause a headline of an undesirable sort. But your answers can matter a great deal. They can be an opportunity to shape the public's sentiments and opinions in a way that helps free government remain good government. Answering such questions – even when they haven't been asked – has in the course of our history given an opportunity for America's greatest statesmen in small or large ways to strengthen the capacity of their fellow citizens to govern themselves. On the other hand, there is hardly a greater mischief that can be done to the people than to give them bad answers to such questions.

In my last letter I took the liberty of questioning the notion, recently espoused by some leading public officials, that America is exceptional because its principles give it a special right and responsibility to lead. This is a confusion, I argued, if an understandable confusion, of a genuine American exceptionalism that is older than America itself – namely, the idea of America as an example to the world – "a city upon a hill," as John Winthrop said to the future Massachusetts Bay colonists. By 1776, when the 13 colonies assumed their separate and equal station among the powers of the earth as the United States of America, they did so proclaiming principles that made America truly exceptional. "We hold these truths to be self-evident," they declared, "that all men are created equal, that they are endowed by their creator with certain inalienable rights," including life, liberty, and the pursuit of happiness. No people on earth had ever based the authority of their laws on such an assertion. So the historic effort to establish government upon this principle was in truth an unprecedented and exceptional – a then unique – experiment in self-government.

As Thomas Jefferson put it in his last surviving letter, written just before he died 50 years to the day after July 4, 1776, the American idea of equality meant "that the mass of mankind has not been born with saddles on their backs, nor a favored few booted and spurred, ready to ride them legitimately, by the grace of God." America was exceptional in founding our politics on what is least exceptional about us, on what we share with all other human beings at all times and in all places, rather than on any accidents of birth or circumstance that separate us. For this reason, Jefferson thought that the principles proclaimed in the Declaration not only gave hope to all Americans but were "grounds of hope for others," everywhere and always.

The experiment of living up to these principles is the American experiment – the effort generation after generation to rise to equality, as Lincoln put it. So long as America remains America, it will be the country first dedicated to this proposition that all men are created equal, and ever aspiring to rise to its demands. Lincoln, echoing Jefferson, called the American idea the "principle of 'Liberty to all' – the principle that clears the *path* for all – gives *hope* to all – and, by consequence, *enterprise*, and *industry* to all."

The American experiment claimed to be an exceptional experiment not only because of its principles, but because conditions here in America were more favorable to the experiment in self-government than anywhere else in the world. The Founders' America really was a land of opportunity as had never been known in the world before. The United States, as the saying then had it, became "the best poor man's country on earth." Ordinary people, secure in their equal liberty and therefore full of hope and enterprise, could farm their own land and enjoy in peace the bread of their labor; and for the first time in human history, they or their children could aspire without limit to great things – even to the Presidency of the

United States. If the experiment in self-government fails here, our Founders thought, that failure might be taken as a strong proof that, contrary to American assertions, human beings are not made to govern themselves.

Just as Jefferson and Lincoln hoped, the example of America has helped spread the blessings of liberty to other peoples. Many countries now claim equality as the principle of their politics. May they live up to those principles, as we hope to do ourselves!

Here in America, when we succeed in living up to our principles, we do something more important than establishing our right to lead. We establish our worthiness to lead, whenever our interest guided by our justice should require. To rise to these principles, we must understand them. And since we are not born understanding them, we arrange as best we can to learn them from one another – sometimes by listening to our politicians talk about our country – and to hand them down to our children. Can there be a more propitious occasion to refresh our understanding than the annual approach of the Fourth of July? Let us return to these themes next week.

OHIO FARMER

No. 20

Novus Ordo Seclorum
July 4, 2011

To the Members of the 112th Congress:

America will always have the honor of being the first nation on earth to dedicate itself to the self-evident truth that all men are created equal, as it did in declaring independence on July 4, 1776. In that dedication truly was created a New Order of the Ages – a Novus Ordo Seclorum as we say on the Great Seal of the United States. Let us take the occasion of this Independence Day to continue our reflections on what this means. What does it tell us about the foundations, forms, and purposes of American politics? What does it require of us – deserve from us?

Lincoln called the idea of equality the central idea of the American political experiment, from which all its other ideas radiate. It is, he wrote, "an abstract truth, applicable to all men and all times"; it is a philosophical idea about human nature and the just relations of each human being to all others. The revolutionary and founding generation of Americans expressed this idea of human equality in a variety of ways. The familiar language of the Declaration of Independence is "that all men are created equal." To express the same idea, the Virginia Declaration of Rights (June 12, 1776) stated that "all men are by nature equally free and independent." The Declaration of the Rights of the Inhabitants of the Commonwealth of Massachusetts (March 2, 1780) stated that "All men are born free and equal."

To say that all men are by nature equal is to say that human beings are not naturally subordinated one to another: Whatever the many differences may be among human beings, no man is by nature a master; no man is by nature a slave. This is what Jefferson's vivid metaphor meant, which we quoted in the last letter: "the mass of mankind has not been born with saddles on their backs, nor a favored few booted and spurred, ready to ride them legitimately, by the grace of God." Of this revolutionary idea, at the heart of the Declaration and at the heart of the American experiment in self-government, Lincoln wrote on the eve of Civil War, "that to-day, and in all coming days, it shall be a rebuke and a stumbling-block to the very harbingers of re-appearing tyranny and oppression." And so it has proven to be: a powerful rebuke and a stumbling block to every form of tyranny and oppression – whether of race, class, or religion, whether home grown or foreign born – that has raised its head over the past two centuries.

Human beings, then, are naturally free as they are naturally equal. It is from this human equality and freedom that the Founders derived the idea that government could only be justly founded on consent. Because human beings are not by nature subordinated to one another – that is, because they are equal and free – their consent must be obtained before any human being may rightfully exercise authority over them. It is the voluntary consent of the people that gives authority to government. Only a being possessing reason – a being who can distinguish right from wrong – is capable of voluntary consent. This is why the deepest root of American politics is in the fact, as Thomas Jefferson put it in the Virginia Statute for Religious Liberty, "that Almighty God hath created the mind free."

Government among free and equal men is formed, the American Founders would say, by social contract or social compact. In the words of the Massachusetts Constitution of 1780: "The body-politic is formed by a voluntary association of individuals: It is a social compact, by which the whole people covenants with each citizen, and each citizen with the whole people." The American body-politic is a voluntary association begun when, in the last words of the Declaration of Independence, "for the support of this Declaration, with a firm Reliance on the Protection of divine Providence, we mutually pledge[d] to each other our Lives, our Fortunes, and our sacred Honor." This is the political community that new citizens enter into when they become citizens. To take on the responsibilities of such citizenship, it is necessary – for citizens old and new – to understand the principles on which this citizenship is based. So it is a useful tradition, as the Fourth of July comes around each year, to reflect again – and again – on the American political principles famously declared to the world on the original Independence Day.

As Thomas Jefferson wrote late in life, in drafting the Declaration of Independence he had not meant to proclaim any "new principles, or new arguments, never before thought of," but merely to express "the American mind." The Declaration contains a stunning summation of the principles of free government; but it was only because the American people already understood these principles that it was possible to establish a government based upon them. Similarly, only if we are capable of understanding these principles will we be able to preserve and perpetuate, maybe even to strengthen and improve, the free institutions – the Novus Ordo Seclorum – that began to arise from them in 1776. For our own sake and for the sake of the cause to which our country was dedicated on that original Fourth of July, let us take this occasion to renew our dedication to that cause and its noble principles. No one else can do it for us. It will do a world of good. And it is a cause worthy of the last full measure of devotion.

Happy Fourth.

OHIO FARMER

No. 21

The American Mind

July 12, 2011

To the Members of the 112th Congress:

We saw in the last letter that the revolutionary principles Americans declared to the world on July 4, 1776 – the principles that gave rise to a New Order of the Ages when, in support of them, the American people pledged their lives, fortunes and sacred honor – were not "new principles…never before thought of." They were principles already well understood by the American people, who were in the midst of a historic conversation about the principles of political freedom, a conversation that gave birth to what Jefferson called "the American mind." The Declaration of Independence expressed in bold American terms the logic of political freedom that had become the common sense of the American people.

One essential ingredient of this logic of freedom, which is still very much part of American common sense, was the idea that, because human beings are equal and free by nature, legitimate government can only arise from the consent of the governed. A nation dedicated to the proposition that all men are created equal will – if circumstances permit – be under a "government of the people, by the people, for the people." In other words, the principle of equality gives rise most naturally to a democratic or republican form of government. James Madison expressed this idea in *Federalist* 39, where he considered whether the government proposed under the new constitution would be "strictly republican." "It is evident," he wrote, "that no other form would be reconcilable with the genius of the people of America…[or] with the fundamental principles of the Revolution."

Because of our conviction that consent is the foundation of legitimate government, we are concerned in every election that the election be fairly conducted, truly expressing the choice or consent of the people. But although consent is the only foundation of legitimate government, it does not follow that all governments founded on consent deserve the respect of freedom's partisans. The Founders did not suppose that a tyranny must be submitted to by a minority just because a majority elected it. That would mean asking those who are to be oppressed by a majority to accept their oppression with equanimity – as the rightful expression of the noble principles of democracy. It would be to tell oppressed peoples everywhere to cease their struggles for their natural rights as soon as they learn they are outnumbered. What could be more slavish?

These days this point has particular relevance to the various uprisings – some apparently supported by majorities – across the Arab world. These uprisings and rebellions are typically against various forms of tyranny, but they often seem to possess the potential to replace one tyranny with another. How would Jefferson's "American mind" think about such human events? It would begin, I think, by acknowledging that majority rule is the natural authoritative expression of the consent of the governed; in the same breath, it would observe that free government is instituted to secure the rights of *all the people*, not just the majority. The very purpose of free government thus sets limits to what even a majority may rightly do.

Jefferson, in his first inaugural address, expressed this idea with characteristic felicity when he urged his countrymen to "bear in mind this sacred principle, that though the will of the majority is in all cases to prevail, that will to be rightful must be reasonable; that the minority possesses their equal rights, which equal law must protect, and to violate would be oppression." The will of the majority must be exercised within the bounds of that moral order which legitimates majority rule itself. A thousand tyrants are no more palatable than one. Majority rule and minority rights are therefore inseparable principles of free government. Being bound to respect minority rights does not detract from the majority's right to rule; it dignifies it. Americans are partisans of free government, but this does not make them partisans of elective despotism, at home or abroad. Oppressive majorities deserve no more respect from us than any other oppressors.

This leads to another ingredient of the logic of political freedom or of American common sense – the idea of "equal law," which Jefferson mentioned in his first inaugural. As we have noted, the idea of human equality and freedom carries with it the recognition of human rationality; it also contains within it recognition of the limits of human rationality. Because human beings are by nature rational beings, one man may not rightly rule over another as he may rightly rule over a non-rational being (a dog or a horse, for example). But also, because no man is all-knowing or all-good – that is, because human reason is limited and fallible and subject to human passions – one human being may never rightly subject himself to the unrestrained will or unlimited power of another. This is what Madison meant when he wrote that "government...[is] the greatest of all reflections on human nature."

> If men were angels [he wrote], no government would be necessary. If angels were to govern men, neither external nor internal controls on government would be necessary. In framing a government which is to be administered by men over men, the great difficulty lies in this: You must first enable the government to control the governed; and in the next place, oblige it to control itself.

Human nature or human equality – the fact that human beings are neither angels nor mindless brutes – gives rise to the idea of constitutional or limited government. This is a political constitution that conforms to the natural constitution of man. Because human beings possess reason, their consent can give rise to legitimate government; because human reason is fallible and subject sometimes to unreasonable passions, human government must be subject to law.

It required much experience, reflection, and study for the American revolutionaries and Founders to equip the American mind so that its common sense might establish free government that would be good government. Their exertions have left a rich legacy to us, making it easier – though never easy! – for us to ensure that America will continue to be what the revolutionaries and Founders rightly thought it was at its inception – "the world's best hope."

OHIO FARMER

No. 22

The Just Powers of Government
July 19, 2011

To the Members of the 112th Congress:

In the last letter, I considered why and how it is that in the American logic of freedom, the just powers of government are derived from the consent of the governed. In this letter, I am concerned with a current development in our politics that threatens dangerously to remove our government from our consent. If the letter seems painfully burdened with acronyms, please forgive the fact as a vice inseparable from the subject.

Several lawsuits have been filed against the Patient Protection and Affordable Care Act (PPACA or "Obamacare") since it was enacted in March 2010. The ones that have worked their way into the federal court system so far contest the law's "individual mandate," which subjects people to monetary fines if they fail or refuse to enroll in a health insurance policy. The lawsuits' question, which the court and the people must consider, is whether the legitimate powers of the federal government respect or traduce the inalienable rights of the people by requiring them to buy a financial product from a private vendor.

One lawsuit against PPACA raises a different and equally important question: Does the law violate the constitutional principle of separation of powers? The Goldwater Institute challenges, specifically, the constitutionality of PPACA's "Independent Payment Advisory Board" (IPAB). The Board is the law's chief mechanism for bending the medical cost curve downward by reducing the growth rate of Medicare outlays to the rate at which the Gross Domestic Product increases, plus one percent. IPAB's 15 members will be appointed by the president and confirmed by the Senate. Since it won't adjust the premiums or deductibles paid by Americans enrolled in Medicare, IPAB's power derives from its mandate to set the rates at which Medicare reimburses doctors for the various services or procedures they perform.

IPAB's power is buttressed by PPACA's extraordinary protections for it, whose constitutionality is at issue. Even though IPAB is an executive branch agency, its "legislative proposals" – the PPACA uses the term repeatedly – become law unless Congress passes a bill that cuts medical spending by an amount equal to the IPAB proposal. They become law, that is, if Congress does nothing. If Congress tries to do something, its alternative can prevail over the IPAB proposal only if the former garners a three-fifths majority in the Senate. The law makes no provision for citizens, such as doctors, to challenge IPAB's determinations administratively or judicially. Furthermore, PPACA asserts the right to dictate what future Congresses may do, and when: IPAB can only be abolished, according to its provisions, by legislation introduced and enacted between February 1, 2017 and August 15, 2017. Even if enacted in that small window, the abolition cannot take effect until 2020.

Peter Orszag, President Obama's director of the Office of Management and Budget at the time PPACA was enacted, said, "I believe [IPAB] is the largest yielding of sovereignty from the Congress since the creation of the Federal Reserve." He was speaking approvingly. Democratic Congressman Pete Stark, who got a 90% rating from the liberal Americans for Democratic Action in 2010, made the same point about IPAB far less fondly, calling it "an unprecedented abrogation of Congressional authority to an unelected, unaccountable body of so-called experts."

In a nation founded upon the principle that governments derive their just powers from the consent of the governed, the decision by Congress to yield so much of its sovereignty to an unelected, unaccountable body is really a decision to yield the people's sovereignty for them. Thus, if PPACA withstands all its challenges in federal courts, an outraged public could elect a ferociously anti-IPAB Congress in 2012 and 2014 – to no avail whatsoever. The Board remains beyond the voters' reach until after the 2016 elections – and then only for a 6½-month period, after which the door slams shut again, bolted against meddling by mere citizens for the duration of the republic.

Like most bad ideas, IPAB is the elaboration of a less bad idea. Its predecessors include such bodies as the Base Realignment and Closure Commission, which drew up lists of military bases for the Pentagon to close, lists that Congress could accept or reject in their entirety, but could not add to or subtract from. If Congress did nothing, the BRAC proposal was enacted.

"Stop us before we pander again," seems to be the legislative principle embedded in these commissions. Or do you think that is an unfair assessment? It seems to me that when Congress voluntarily surrenders some of its legislative power to a commission, it is admitting that rendering good government as good politics is too daunting and risky. Wise and judicious policies, you seem to be saying, might prove to be too hard to explain to the voters; or they might be criticized by a political opponent in a 30-second television ad. Better, then, to leave the tough calls to commissioners who derive their powers from the consent of the governed in arcane, impenetrable ways.

Once entrenched, it is doubtful that government of the people by the commissions will ever be dislodged. The threat comes not only from the prospect that the commissioners' power will tend to corrupt them, but from the citizenry's passive acquiescence in the attenuation of their own sovereignty. At the heart of the American experiment is the belief that democratic government can also be good government. If it turns out that only philosopher-kings, benevolent dictators, or unaccountable experts can provide good government, the experiment will have failed.

IPAB, then, is not just outrageous, it is contemptible. By out-sourcing its legislative power Congress is saying that it doesn't trust the people to make wise decisions, and doesn't trust itself to explain such decisions to them. If IPAB stands unchallenged, the American polity will have suffered a grievous blow.

OHIO FARMER

No. 23

Willful Majorities or Constitutional Majorities
July 26, 2011

To the Members of the 112th Congress:

The 2012 elections loom in the near distance, and the presidential race could well be tighter than in 2008. So pundits, professors, and some politicians express concern, as they do every four years, that the candidate who wins the majority of the national popular vote might not win a majority of the Electoral College vote. I know this is a mathematical possibility; I think it has happened four times in 56 presidential elections. But does this possibility somehow violate the principles of fundamental fairness, disenfranchise the American voter, and bring disgrace to American democracy? This is what is alleged every four years by those who advocate overturning the Electoral College.

By the testimony of the Framers of the Constitution themselves, designing the office of the presidency was the most difficult task they faced. They began with the idea of having an executive chosen by the national legislature; they considered having him chosen by state legislatures, state governors, directly by the people, by special electors, and by various combinations of these methods. The mode of selection was a question inseparable from other questions: what powers to be granted to the office, the term of office, the question of reeligibility, whether the executive should be single or plural. These questions were also related to the foundations, powers, and structures of the other branches. And all these questions were related to the overarching question of how to construct a government that would best secure the safety and happiness of the people.

After weeks of deliberations, the Framers came up with a mode of selecting the president that has managed to provide for the relatively seamless transition of government for over two hundred years. Aside from this commendable record, the Electoral College seems to have other desirable effects. It discourages regional parties, moderating local interests by inducing them to seek a national and federal base; it provides protections for minorities, beneficently affects the character of majorities formed in selecting a president, and makes the president beholden not to the passions of a numerical majority, but to the Constitution. In all these ways, the history of the Electoral College has justified Alexander Hamilton's conclusion that, if this mode of selecting a president is not perfect, it is nonetheless "excellent."

Dismissing all these interesting ingredients of our constitutional politics, opponents of the Electoral College demand simple national majoritarianism in the selection of our presidents. But they recognize that they do not themselves have the constitutional majority necessary to amend the Constitution. So, with no apparent sense of irony – dubbing themselves now the "National Popular Vote" movement (NPV) – they have devised a way of nullifying the Electoral College by substituting a constitutionally dubious, potentially minority vote for the constitutional majority required in the amendment process. The NPV has launched a movement to persuade states representing 270 electoral votes – the number it takes to win the presidency under the current electoral college system – to agree through a "compact" to award all their electoral votes to the presidential candidate who wins the popular vote nationwide.

Hawaii, Illinois, Maryland, Massachusetts, New Jersey, Vermont, Washington state, and the District of Columbia have already agreed to this compact. A bill to make California part of the compact (AB 459) has just been approved by the California legislature and awaits the signature of Governor Jerry Brown. If California's 55 electoral votes are to be added to the compacting states, they will be about half way to the 270 votes needed to activate the compact. In each of the states participating in the compact, the majority vote of the states' citizens is to be dismissed – or, actually, reversed – if it disagrees with the majority vote of the nations' citizens. If a candidate wins a state but loses the national popular vote, this compact requires the state to allocate its electoral votes not to the candidate who wins in the state, but to the candidate who loses – some democracy!

The NPV seeks constitutional authority for its effort in Article II, Section 1, of the Constitution, which says regarding the election of the president: "Each State shall appoint, in such Manner as the Legislature thereof may direct, a Number of Electors, equal to the whole Number of Senators and Representatives to which the State may be entitled in the

Congress." Their ambitious reading of this article shows the respect for the Constitution that one would expect from a movement seeking to undermine the constitutional requirements for elections by circumventing the constitutional requirements for amendments.

As to Article I, Section 10, of the Constitution, dealing with interstate compacts, the National Popular Vote movement dismisses it as irrelevant. This is what the Constitution says: "No State shall, *without the consent of Congress*... enter into Agreement or Compact with another State, or with a foreign Power, or engage in War, unless actually invaded, or in such imminent Danger as will not admit of delay" (emphasis added). But the NPV argues that their "compact" is none of Congress's business. Do you think presidential elections are none of your business?

We Americans are a constitutional people. From the beginning, we insisted that our politics must be answerable to the consent of the governed, and we devised constitutional ways of constructing and shaping our authoritative consent so that our choices would not reflect mere willful majorities but would reflect the cool and deliberate and just sense of the community. If we are to change the electoral system in a fundamental way, we should engage, not in constitutional trickery, but in the constitutional deliberation provided for the purpose – as we have done several times in the past. We should always be skeptical of attempts to circumvent provisions very deliberately put into the Constitution, just because a loud interest group of the moment finds them inconvenient. Where populist passion seeks to circumvent the Constitution in order to remove a constitutional check on populist passion, we should be all the more skeptical.

OHIO FARMER

No. 24

The Sense of the People
August 1, 2011

To the Members of the 112th Congress:

In the negotiations over increasing the national debt ceiling, one fact is so obvious it has barely been mentioned: America has a government that can be, and currently is, divided. A Democratic president and Senate majority leader sit at the table with a Republican Speaker of the House.

Were the configuration otherwise, as it was between the 2008 and 2010 elections when Democrats controlled the House of Representatives as well as the Senate and the presidency, the debt ceiling debate would probably not be taking place at all. When Democratic majorities in both houses of Congress passed an increase in the debt ceiling in 2010, Republican legislators made some critical speeches but the bill moved swiftly to President Obama's desk for signature.

The possibility of divided government inheres in a constitutional republic where both houses of a bicameral legislature and the head of the executive branch are all elected by the people, but not by the same people at the same time. As our civics textbooks teach us, each Representative is elected for two years by voters in one of the 435 congressional districts. Senators are elected every six years, state-by-state. Because those six-year terms are staggered, only one third of the Senate faces the voters in any given election, while the entire membership of the House does. Presidents are elected every four years by the entire, constitutionally organized, national electorate.

Divisions like America's could never occur in a parliamentary democracy where the people elect the entire legislature at once. The party that wins a majority forms a government, and the prime minister – a member of the legislature, as are all the cabinet members – submits legislation that his party invariably passes. Such systems have been described as "dictatorships punctuated by elections."

More than a century ago, the American progressives began their historic assault on our constitutional system, yearning for the clarity and dispatch of a parliamentary system. Woodrow Wilson, for example, sought sweeping reforms that would "make self-government among us a straightforward thing of simple method, single, unstinted power, and clear responsibility." H.L. Mencken, Wilson's contemporary, offered a less celebratory expression of the same idea: "Democracy is the theory that the common people know what they want, and deserve to get it good and hard."

One strand of the political philosophy woven into the Constitution is that sometimes the people *don't* know what they want, and other times they think they do, only to wind up regretting their "settled" opinions after some reassessment. The Constitution's authors believed, as one of them stated in *Federalist* 63, that "where the concurrence of separate and dissimilar bodies [such as the House and Senate] is required in every public act," the republic is best prepared to navigate "particular moments in public affairs when the people…may call for measures which they themselves will afterwards be the most ready to lament and condemn." The objective, as we have had several occasions to observe in these letters, is that "the cool and deliberate sense of the community" will "ultimately prevail."

Each party would clearly prefer to deal with the debt ceiling, and the nation's long-term fiscal problems, on its own terms, with both houses of Congress and the presidency under its control. If the Democrats had their way, that would mean higher taxes, especially on the rich; more borrowing, especially until the unemployment rate is much lower; and few spending cuts, especially from domestic programs. If Republicans controlled both ends of Pennsylvania Avenue, they would emphasize spending cuts, especially to domestic programs; less borrowing; tax reforms to apply lower, simpler tax rates to a broader, more vigorous tax base; and regulatory reforms to stimulate economic growth.

Which approach best reflects "the will of the people"? That may be a question that doesn't, at least for the moment, really have an answer. It's not as though either party's philosophy has been hidden over the past years, or undergone profound changes. The voters knew what they were getting when they gave Republicans control over all the federal elected branches from 2002 to 2006, and then when they disliked the results, and chose to check a Republican president with a Democratic House and Senate. The voters knew, or should have known, what they were getting when they empowered Democrats to run everything in 2008, and then again two years later when they decided to return the Republicans to a majority in the House to curtail the Democrats' policy-making latitude.

It would be fair to say, in other words, that the electorate has serious misgivings about both the Democrats' "big government" approach and the Republicans' "limited government" one. After signing up for either, the people quickly succumb to buyer's remorse and avail themselves of the opportunity to weaken or impede the "mandate" they conferred an election or two ago.

Americans didn't used to hedge their political bets this way. From 1900 to 1980 the White House, Senate, and House of Representatives were controlled by the same party for a total of 56 years, 70% of the time. Those 56 years included 14 consecutive years of Democratic control, from 1932 to 1946, when the New Deal was launched, and eight more from 1960 to 1968, which saw the beginning of the Great Society.

By the time the ballots from the 2012 election are counted, the same party will have controlled both houses of Congress and the presidency for only 8 of the preceding 32 years, or 25% of the time. This new era, in which divided government is the rule rather than the exception, was ushered in by the election of Ronald Reagan to the presidency, and GOP victories that gave the party its first Senate majority since 1954.

It's hard to believe that these two developments – the emergence of a credible conservative opposition to the governmental activism promoted by FDR and LBJ, and the beginning of a long era in which partisan majorities are rare and transient – are coincidental. Roosevelt and Johnson spoke to and for an American majority that liked the benefactions big government bestowed. Reagan spoke to and for a majority grown skeptical about the taxes, borrowing, and regulatory intrusions big government required.

That skepticism was sufficient to slow the growth of big government, but not to dismantle the New Deal/Great Society. For the past 31 years the American people have straddled an untenable position: voting in favor of most of what big government does, but against most of what big government requires. The debate in Washington over the debt ceiling is an echo of the debate, across America, over the proper scope and cost of government, a debate that seeks a resolution it has not yet found. The cool and deliberate sense of the national community will ultimately prevail, but it must first settle on one or the other of two alternatives that are fundamentally opposed.

OHIO FARMER

No. 25

Words and Politics
August 9, 2011

To the Members of the 112th Congress:

Everyone across the political spectrum has been rightly celebrating the one grace note of the recent protracted battle in Washington over raising the debt ceiling – the moment when Arizona Representative Gabrielle Giffords appeared on the House floor, still recovering from her grievous wounds, to cast a vote on the climactic legislation.

Giffords' welcome presence revived discussion of "civility" in our political life, a respectable term that had been deployed in the most uncivil way against raucous Tea Party activists in the moments after Giffords' shooting in January. Then in the heat of the debt ceiling battle, leading journalists and office holders who have been most sanctimonious about civility called the Tea Party "terrorists." It should go without saying that civility is important to "civil society," but it should be equally noted that a high rhetorical pitch is especially endemic to democratic forms of government that put a premium on serious public argument over essential questions of justice and policy. There is an opportunity here for the Tea Party to turn this attack on its head, and to break new rhetorical ground in Washington.

The fervency of Tea Party rhetoric about potentially tyrannical government is nothing especially new or different in American politics; nor is there anything new in critics using extreme language to attack the Tea Party's supposed extremism. John Adams and Thomas Jefferson, who first fought each other with extreme bitterness and then conducted one of the most edifying correspondences between statesmen in human history, might well find the current discussion of civility in politics to be frivolous and unserious. Jefferson's supporters charged Adams with wanting to refasten British monarchy on America, while Adams' supporters alleged that Jefferson's election would mean the importation of the French guillotine and the blood of revolutionary terror running through every American town.

Our tender censors of political discourse would exhaust their vocabulary of outrage if faced with the harshness of public discourse at earlier periods of our history, not to mention the ways the hot tempers of political argument spilled over into actual violence. The famous duel between Alexander Hamilton and Aaron Burr was a rare but not unheard of thing in the early years of our republic; as nastily as our politicians can speak today, at least no one has been assaulted in a Capitol chamber like Senator Charles Sumner in 1856, when Rep. Preston Brooks beat Sumner savagely with a cane in the heat of the bitter debate over the Kansas-Nebraska Act. Nor have we seen mobs descending on newspaper offices and shooting editors as occurred in Alton, Illinois in the famous case of Elijah Lovejoy in 1837 – the event which inspired the teaching of Lincoln's first great speech at the Young Men's Lyceum the following year.

It may not simply be a lack of historical perspective, however, that has led to the current focus on civility in politics. There is no doubt that changes in modern mass media have amplified our political discord. In two generations we have gone from a media world of mostly print and radio to 24-hour television news and the always-on, unfiltered anarchy of the Internet. Perhaps this may amount to a qualitative change in the effect of political rhetoric, just as the invention of movable type 500 years ago was a socially and politically disruptive mass media technology. Like movable type and cheap books five centuries ago, our all-encompassing high tech mass media world is here to stay. As the kids say, deal with it.

There is one aspect of political rhetoric, however, that office holders have within their power to change, and that change might help remove the sense many citizens have that our political class is remote from us. When elected officials arrive in Washington, they very quickly pick up a way of talking that is not found in any other walk of life. It comes in two forms. First is the language of "comity," the way in which our senators and representatives habitually refer to their bitter political opponents as "my good friend from the great state of Colorado," and so forth. In a few cases, this language expresses a true friendship across party lines, but it is usually a lie, and everyone watching on C-SPAN knows it is a lie.

This language probably is an import from the British parliamentary procedure of referring to the "right honorable gentleman from Blaby," or some other specific constituency, in the House of Commons debates, but the formality of assuming honor in one's opponents is a different thing than asserting *friendship* where none exists. This language of comity probably serves a useful purpose in keeping political discourse more temperate, but why not drop the pretense and use more neutral language – "the representative from New Jersey," "the senator from New Mexico," even "the honorable representative from New Jersey"?

Second, elected officials in Washington always lapse quickly into a Capitol Hill jargon that subtly reinforces some bad tendencies of modern government in ways that are almost unnoticed, but which contribute to the peoples' dislike of our political class. Members of the House, in particular, speak of "my constituents" back home in the district. But speaking of your fellow citizens as "constituents" abets the notion that your primary job is to pry as many goodies from Washington as you can for your "constituents." If the Tea Party caucus really wants to mark themselves out as a different kind of political force, they should think about banishing the term "constituents," and instead speak of *citizens* – a term which emphasizes our political equality. (By the way, like the "right honorable gentleman" usage, this particular formulation is also an import from Britain, and it conveys the sense that our elected officials are our *masters* more than our *representatives*.)

In a similar vein, Tea Party caucus members should try not to use Capitol Hill jargon, which most members, especially new ones, adopt to convey the air of insider-sophistication. Some of the special terms of art on Capitol Hill, like "budget reconciliation" and so forth, are unavoidable, but other phrases could benefit from Churchill's rule of linguistic simplification. For example, don't speak of using an "expedited process" to consider budget issues; instead, say "fast track." Then the fact that nothing is ever fast in Congress will be revealed with some embarrassment for the process-oriented insiders.

If Tea Partiers actually speak differently as well as thinking differently, it will mark them out even more as a reforming force in Washington. And if they do that, their critics will continue to call them names, mostly short, non-jargony names that are easy to make out. That will be another sign of their impact.

OHIO FARMER

No. 26

War and the American Character
August 16, 2011

To the Members of the 112th Congress:

Can a free, democratic people possess the martial virtues needed to defend their interests in the hard world? Early observers of the American republic doubted it. Some believed that a commercial people like the Americans were not cut out for war. Some thought that the American Constitution and federalism further disabled the country from waging war successfully.

That great student of America, Alexis de Tocqueville, thought that "The most important of all the actions that can mark the life of a people is war." (We are inclined to think that the most important of a people's actions necessarily take place in the peace achieved by war, but let's set that aside for another letter.) Tocqueville's famous study of America had led him in the 1830s to the conclusion that "in the midst of a great war," confusions in America's federal and state constitutions would cause either liberty or the American Union to crumble. American republicanism, he thought, would be saved only by geography: far from the rest of the dangerous world, it was the "great good fortune of the United States…not to have hit upon a federal constitution that enables it to endure a great war, but rather to be so situated that it need not fear such a war."

The many failures of American arms during the War of 1812 seemed to have validated Tocqueville's view, but only a decade after he wrote, American success during the war against Mexico suggested that there may be more to be said on the question. Americans are, indeed, a people who prefer peace and the prosperity that comes with it, but if our history so far is any indication, we seem to be a people who are not necessarily spoiled by those conditions. When aroused to action, Americans have traditionally responded with alacrity and courage, as they did after Pearl Harbor and again after 9/11. And contrary to Tocqueville's expectations, the Federal

Constitution has enabled the United States to wage war successfully without destroying liberty at home.

We approach the tenth anniversary of the terrorist attacks of September 11, 2001. America has been waging war for a decade. Our experience in this war confirms a long-standing conviction of the American people. From the time of the American Revolution, Americans have acted on the fundamental belief that the virtues needed for war are not the exclusive property of a professional military establishment – a "standing army" – but can be found in the citizens of the republic at large. Today's American military is clearly "professional" in the sense that service members are long-term volunteers, but those who serve understand themselves to be every bit the citizen soldiers their forebears were during World War II. This is a force of republican citizens motivated by a deep sense of duty and loyalty to their fellow citizens.

After 9/11, many Americans who could have avoided military service chose to enlist in the military and to fight the wars on which the United States has embarked over the past ten years. It is a tribute to the character of Americans – citizens of all backgrounds – that many chose to forego comfort, safety, and livelihood to engage America's enemies.

The cost has been high. Nearly 4500 Americans have died in Iraq and another nearly 1200 have given the last full measure of devotion in Afghanistan. In the most recent war news, details continue to emerge of the loss of 30 Americans, including 17 Navy SEALs, in a helicopter crash in Afghanistan. Many thousands more have been wounded. Yet even as casualties were rising during the darkest days in Iraq before the "surge" took effect, the services – including those whose members routinely face the greatest danger in the kind of war we are now fighting, the Army and Marines – were meeting their recruiting requirements while retaining large numbers of those eligible to leave the service. These numbers speak eloquently to the martial character of the American people.

The United States is fortunate to be defended by such men as the SEALs who gave their lives in Afghanistan. The quality of today's American military as a whole is extraordinary, and these SEALs and the other "special operators" like them are by consensus the very "best of the best." We mourn their deaths – and the deaths of all who serve the good cause of our country. In honor to this cause, let us mourn them as the heroes they are, and not treat them as some in the country once treated those who served in Vietnam: as "victims."

Our warriors, brought to manhood in the bosom of the American Republic, understand – as we their fellow citizens sometimes forget – that war will always be with us. Civilized peoples will need to be prepared for war so long as savagery and barbarism exist in the world. We can defeat the barbarians and savages when they threaten, but, human nature being what it is, they will always arise among us again in one form or another.

So long as there are people who will kill for gain and power, America will need soldiers who will kill to stop them. But this requires honesty about war and its costs. When we send our fellow citizens into war we must have a clear idea of what we are asking them to do, and must do all in our power to equip them to succeed. Above all, we must do our part to keep the country they serve worthy of their sacrifices.

OHIO FARMER

No. 27

In Search of Monsters
August 23, 2011

To the Members of the 112th Congress:

"Preventing mass atrocities and genocide is a core national security interest and a core moral responsibility of the United States." This is the first sentence in President Obama's recently issued *Presidential Study Directive on Mass Atrocities*. Is it true?

It seems that there have always been, and until human nature changes there will always be, monstrous tyrants in the world doing monstrous things to anyone they can get in the grip of their claws. Whole nations seem capable of becoming bloodthirsty mobs. Some rather nasty tyrants have been in the headlines lately. Presumably Americans, who don't like tyranny of any degree and who began our progress in the world proclaiming the natural right to overthrow tyrants, are especially opposed to tyranny that is atrocious and genocidal. We could probably get 100% of sane Americans to agree that it is desirable to prevent it. But does this make preventing it a "core national security interest" and a "core moral responsibility" of the country?

If men were angels there would be no atrocities to trouble us, but until men become angels, to implement this Directive will require endless American intervention across the sinful and suffering world. America would have to become the "universal landlord," to use a colorful Shakespearean phrase, and this would be neither morally desirable nor strategically feasible, even assuming we were determined to exert all our means to this end. If – unmindful of these moral and strategic truths – we actually meant what we say in the Directive, we would need urgently and radically to increase American spending on our armed forces. We are certainly not going to do that. To the contrary, the President and his entire administration have taken pains to make clear that they intend to reduce American military power. The President issued the Directive at the very time when he was emphatically making known his willingness to cut

American defense spending drastically as part of his domestic negotiations over the debt ceiling. So, we do not mean what we say in this Directive, and everyone can see that. America is announcing its obligation to intervene to prevent evil in the world at the very same time that it is diminishing its ability to do anything about it. This is not "moral responsibility" but the height of moral irresponsibility. It is moralistic boastfulness.

Given America's deteriorating defense posture, the President's Directive seems perfectly calculated to achieve moral bankruptcy in the eyes of the world to complement our actual bankruptcy at home. From the victims of tyrants and their sympathizers it will bring resentment as they see us giving mere lip service to our moralistic commitment. From the tyrants – who are not in the habit of paying heed to weakness – it will bring increasing contempt for our boastful limp-wristed moralizing that speaks loudly and carries no stick.

The President's Directive also represents a further subordination of American foreign policy to the dictates of international institutions, especially the United Nations. There is nothing morally responsible about submitting America's actions in the world to the judgment of this body. Many of its influential members are the very tyrannies committing the atrocities the President wants to make pronouncements about.

There is an old saying about the world of nations. In that world, "the strong do what they will; the weak suffer what they must." This is not a cynical principle, but a candid observation of the facts. It is an expression of moral and strategic modesty. When you are weak, you are in no position to prevent injustices in the world, even injustices to yourself. If America wants to do any good in the world, for itself or anyone else, it is paramount that we be strong. Thus in its infancy, when the United States was weak, George Washington in his famous Farewell Address looked forward to a time when America would be strong enough to have "command of its own fortunes," and when "we may choose peace or war, as our interest, guided by justice, shall counsel."

Within the memory of the older generation in America, the United States became the most powerful nation on Earth, and it remains so. But this is no cause for such boastful and empty pronouncements as the President's Directive. Especially as we recklessly fritter away the strength we have acquired with such effort and good fortune.

If we might more modestly suggest what is "our core moral responsibility," to ourselves and to mankind, we would say as we did in an earlier letter: It is to succeed in our own experiment in freedom. If we can show by the enduring success of our experiment that free government can be good government, this will be the greatest benefit Americans can bestow on their fellow human beings – our own political well being will be a constant act of philanthropy.

Americans should intervene in the world when intervening enhances the prospects of the American experiment. To commit to more than that betrays America's national security interest and our core moral responsibility to ourselves and our fellow human beings. Much better than the boastful posturing of the President's Directive are the modest words of John Quincy Adams: America "goes not abroad, in search of monsters to destroy. She is the well-wisher to the freedom and independence of all [but]…the champion and vindicator only of her own." If we vindicate our own freedom by securing it and using it well, it will be, as it has been from the beginning, a blessing and an inspiration to the world. It is as true today as it was when newly elected President Thomas Jefferson said it in his first inaugural: we are "the world's best hope."

OHIO FARMER

No. 28

Constitutional Lines
August 30, 2011

To the Members of the 112th Congress:

We have observed in these letters that the recent debt ceiling debate reflected deep divisions in Washington, D.C., but that those divisions, in turn, reflected the citizenry's ambivalence about how big government should be, how much it should do, and how much it should tax, borrow, and regulate. The first phase of the debt ceiling debate ended with legislation to raise the nation's legal borrowing authority by $900 billion and to cut planned federal spending over the next decade by a little more than that amount. Thus, Congress and the President achieved Speaker of the House John Boehner's goal to match any debt ceiling increase, at least dollar-for-dollar, by deficit reductions.

The legislation also sets in motion a second phase, where a "super committee" of six members of the House of Representatives (three from each party) and six senators (also three from each party) will endeavor to reduce the nation's deficit spending over the next ten years by a further $1.5 trillion. If the committee agrees on a plan by November 23, 2011, Congress approves it in an up-or-down vote without the possibility of offering amendments by December 23, 2011, and the President signs it, the debt ceiling will be increased by $1.5 trillion. If the committee can't agree on a plan, or submits one the Congress votes down or the President vetoes, the debt ceiling will be increased by $1.2 trillion, and automatic reductions of federal spending by the same amount over the next decade will take effect – spending cuts evenly divided between discretionary domestic programs and national defense spending.

It is remarkable that, three years after the Democrats' across-the-board victories in the 2008 elections, deficit reduction has become the top item on the national political agenda. The most important cause of this change in the political weather is the emergence of the Tea Party movement, which took shape in 2009 and propelled Republican gains in the elections of 2010. That movement remains disparate – it has no headquarters, no single leader, and no agreed upon platform. Yet some core ideas do connect all of the Tea Party's factions and actions. One friendly observer described the Tea Party essence as "populist constitutionalism," since its "divergent groups agree that the federal government has, over the last several decades, stepped further and further outside of the bounds of the Constitution." Some of the movement's prominent figures describe themselves as "constitutional conservatives."

The endeavor to re-establish limits to the government's sphere of action and authority is highly laudable, and fully consistent with the logic and spirit of the American founding. That undertaking will, however, be an intellectual challenge. Reasonable patriots may disagree about the location of the line the authors of the Constitution drew separating what the government may do from what it must not do. They may disagree, as well, about whether the logic of the Constitution countenances informal adjustments to the location of the government's boundaries over time, or demands formal adjustments only, using one of the procedures for amending the Constitution specified in its fifth article.

For example, the power of Congress to declare war, specified in Article I, has fallen into disuse. America hasn't declared war against any nation since 1941, yet has been involved in a number of wars over the past 70 years, some of them large and prolonged. Does constitutional conservatism, rightly understood, entail retroactively designating all of these wars – including Korea, Vietnam, Operation Desert Storm, Iraq, and Afghanistan – illegitimate for never having been formally declared? If so, then either Congress must declare war to authorize future martial actions, or the nation must amend the Constitution to give explicit legitimacy to the kinds of authorizations Congress *has* come to rely on, such as the Tonkin Gulf resolution that was the legal basis for the war in Vietnam. If not, then resolutions and authorizations that fall short of formal declarations of war have acquired a de facto constitutionality: They aren't mentioned in the Constitution, seem not to have been envisioned or favored by the Constitution's authors, have not been the subject of any constitutional amendment, yet have gained acceptance as the way the federal government arrives at decisions about military actions.

The fact that there are disputes about the location of the line between what the government may and may not do, and about whether that line is bright and tight, or wide with shades of gray, does not invalidate the constitutional conservative argument that erasing any such line renders America a very different kind of republic. James Q. Wilson, one of the preeminent American political scientists of the last half century, helps us understand this. The ultimate meaning of the triumph of the New Deal, according to him, is the collapse of the "legitimacy barrier." Since its fall, he argued, "political conflict [has taken] a very different form. New programs need not await the advent of a crisis or an extraordinary majority, because no program is any longer 'new' – it is seen, rather, as an extension, a modification, or an enlargement of something the government is already doing. Since there is virtually nothing the government has not tried to do, there is little it cannot be asked to do."

The correct label for the alternative to limited government is not big government, but unlimited government. The destruction of all legitimacy barriers creates a new constitutional logic in which government grows, not just very big, but limitlessly big. All the forces – political, economic, and judicial – that might constrain it are rendered ineffectual.

This deformation of our republic has gone on so long, and acquired so much inertial strength, that the Tea Party movement's mission is politically as well as intellectually audacious. We have had occasion to note in these letters Abraham Lincoln's argument that "public sentiment is everything" in American democracy: "With public sentiment, nothing can fail; without it nothing can succeed. Consequently, he who molds public sentiment goes deeper than he who enacts statutes or pronounces decisions. He makes statutes and decisions possible or impossible to be executed."

The ultimate goal of constitutional conservatism is to mold public sentiment into a broad, durable consensus in favor of rebuilding legitimacy barriers in American government. This is not a task that will be accomplished by one legislative fight over the debt ceiling, or in one or two election cycles. Conservatives, constitutional and otherwise, sometimes speak as though the establishment and perpetuation of the New Deal is the result of some kind of coup d'état. The fact is, we have this bloated government because we, the people, have shown our favor to the expansion of government's activities far more reliably than to their contraction. The success of constitutional conservatism will depend on exercising the statesmanship that carefully leads the people to set aside their acquired tolerance for a government that purports to have a program for every problem, and rediscover their older apprehensions that any government strong enough to give you anything you want is also strong enough to take away anything you have.

OHIO FARMER

No. 29

Changing Direction
September 6, 2011

To the Members of the 112th Congress:

Much good has been done in Washington recently. I do not refer to the details of the debt reduction agreement, some of which we have already noted, but to the change it signifies – a change of course for the country. Turning around a fleet of aircraft carriers is child's play compared to turning around the ship of state, but I believe we see before our eyes the signs of a great, ponderous movement of America in the right direction. We owe this hopeful movement largely to the determination of the constitutional conservatives within the GOP and to the good judgment of the new Speaker of the House of Representatives.

If you wonder why liberals are in a funk, why the President's approval ratings are hitting rock-bottom, why he signed off on the debt reduction agreement in virtual secrecy, why he is being criticized openly by progressives and even being compared to the feckless Jimmy Carter, why there is disarray within the Democratic Party, you need look no further than to those who elected a GOP majority in the House, the courage of the Representatives who were elected, and the prudence of Speaker Boehner. He got almost everything he could reasonably have hoped for in the debt reduction agreement, producing the most radical reorientation of government in our generation. President Obama and the Democrats agreed to massive spending cuts, with more to come, and no tax increases.

This a strategic and tactical disaster for the progressives and the Democrats, but, far more important is that the debt ceiling debate exposed what Speaker Boehner calls "the arrogant habits of Washington" and opened fundamental political and constitutional questions. The debate in Washington is shifting away from the favors government might bestow to the question of the proper role of government. As satisfying as his political victory must be, Boehner should be most encouraged by the opening now created to begin a broader conversation about big-government liberalism – really limitless-government liberalism – and why it must be reined in.

If those who brought this about remain resolute, there is a chance of bringing American government back within the bounds of the Constitution. Boehner and his Republican supporters are beginning to disprove an assumption held by progressives and liberals (and the media) since the New Deal: that government will always grow in size and scope, that all spending increases are permanent. This is a historic change, a movement toward re-establishing public recognition that there are some things it is better not to ask government to do [see Ohio Farmer Letter "Constitutional Lines"]. The ear of the public is now listening to the argument for limited self-government. If their elected representatives and other public leaders can continue to explain why limiting the power of the federal government is a good thing, we have the opportunity to form public sentiment into a durable governing consensus.

During the debate over the debt ceiling, much was said about how our government is so divided that it is dysfunctional, and how the solution to the perceived problem is bipartisanship. Some went so far as to assert that the purpose of government is efficiency. Others argued or implied that a parliamentary system would be preferable to the constitutional one we have. After all, there are problems in the world, and our government is not solving them.

We continue to hear such assertions on a daily basis, but they miss the point. The fact is that our Constitution builds in division [see Ohio Farmer Letter, "The Sense of the People"]; it deliberately makes it difficult to form majorities, and even more difficult to hold them. The Constitution's purpose is not efficiency. Our constitutional government is not unified, as is, for example, the British Parliamentary regime (we note in passing that the British prime minister speaks for the government, while our president speaks for his administration, only a part of the government). With its federalism, separation of powers, bicameralism, and other inventions of prudence, our republican regime intentionally divides, checks, and balances power, so that,

> in the extended republic of the United States, and among
> the great variety of interests, parties, and sects which it
> embraces, a coalition of a majority of the whole society

could seldom take place on any other principles than
those of justice and the general good.

Of course, this means that large issues cannot be quickly resolved.
Changing direction in our constitutional regime is wonderfully and
deliberately complicated.

The easiest and quickest way to form *part* of our constitutional
majority is through the House of Representatives. Should we be surprised
that the new majority in the House – formed but two years into the
majority that won the presidency and both branches of Congress for the
Democrats – should assert itself? And should we be surprised that the
President's response is to ask this newest majority to become bipartisan
(read "Democrat")? Politics is not rocket science.

The election of Ronald Reagan in 1980, along with the first
Republican Senate majority since 1954, alerted us to divisions in the
American electorate that had been muffled during the prior 50 years. Since
then noisy debates have continued, with Republicans losing the Senate,
then regaining it, losing the presidency, then winning the House, then
losing it, and so on. We will need more than a few electoral cycles – and
continued conversation and persuasion from the Republicans – to see
whether the determination to limit government will take root in public
opinion and become the principle of a new governing majority in
American politics. In the meantime, let the divisions and the arguments
for and against constitutional limits continue. Public reflection and
constitutional deliberation is our strength, not our weakness.

OHIO FARMER

No. 30

Regime of Liberty
September 8, 2011

To the Members of the 112th Congress:

9/11 changed everything: so many have said. But as we reflect on that day, it is good to recall what has not changed in the ten intervening years.

Seasons have come and gone. Leaves have turned color in New England's fall; flowers bloomed in the desert southwest with the spring rain. Snow has piled high in the western mountains and filled rivers and reservoirs. Drought has beset new areas, as it ended in others. Torrential rains have brought flood waters; hurricanes have wreaked havoc; earthquakes shaken the West, the East, and points in between. And the land has brought forth harvest after harvest.

Couples have fallen in love; babies have been born; the young have aged; some of the old, the famous and the unknown alike, have passed away, disease and time taking their toll. But as always, the population of the United States has increased steadily, by more than 30 million. Over 11 million people not born citizens became citizens. All of them, like the millions who have come to us one way or another throughout our history, were drawn by the hope of a better life.

We have held two Presidential elections; over 130 elections to the Senate; over 1700 elections to the House of Representatives; and almost countless elections of Governors, state legislatures, judges, district attorneys, sheriffs, school boards, municipal commissions, and numerous other offices of public trust. Some of these elections were barely contested, others bitterly fought, all part of the oldest continuing tradition of democratic politics known to history.

All of these events and many others have unfolded since 9/11, following a pattern unbroken since our Republic came into existence. They manifest the unending concerns of the American people and of the republican government of, for, and by the people that has been ours for over 200 years.

Like floods, hurricanes and droughts, enemies remain part of our life as a people. Among our current foes are those who oppose us because they do not accept the idea of the sovereignty of the people. Only God, they believe, can be sovereign or all-powerful. God must rule, therefore, not the will of the people. Calling the people sovereign is blasphemous, and blasphemers must be punished or destroyed.

Americans know that on this earth the rule of God always means only the rule of men, who claim to act in God's name and with his unlimited power and act merely in their own self-interest. Americans reject such tyranny. They long ago concluded that an all-powerful God may be disappointed in what His creatures do but could not be threatened by their exercise of His gift of freedom. We suspect that those who kill and destroy in the name of a supposedly threatened God actually kill and destroy to defend their own privileges or their fragile sense of self-righteousness.

In attacking the rule of the people, our current enemies are like those we have confronted and defeated before. Nazis and Marxists similarly disparaged the sovereignty of the people, in favor of rule by a supposed master race or master class. Not only did these former enemies disparage American principles, they disdained the American people. They thought us cowards or too soft and divided to defend ourselves. Our current foes made the same mistake.

It is understandable that our enemies underestimate the resolve and power of the people. We do on occasion ourselves. But when we do, we should recall what Thomas Jefferson understood, something else that has not changed. A regime resting on the sovereignty of the people, a regime of liberty, will release immense energy and creative force. More important, only such a regime can satisfy the age-old longing for justice – a human longing that will not be denied. That is the true source of our power and our resilience. It is in the light of this fact that we should contemplate the demands of peoples across the Middle East, especially the young, for governments based on the sovereignty of the people. A sign of the weakness of our current enemies, of their impending defeat, is not their death but the rejection of their ideas by their own children.

As for ourselves, we should remember that government of, for, and by the people has never been easy, but it is best. And it will endure and prosper, as will the people it serves.

OHIO FARMER

No. 31

Congress and the Constitution

September 13, 2011

To the Members of the 112th Congress:

Constitution Day approaches, the day on which we annually commemorate the signing of the Constitution on September 17, 1787, in Independence Hall in Philadelphia. Americans – constitutional people that we are – should celebrate. After declaring our independence in 1776, the first action that "We the People" took was to give ourselves constitutions in our various states. Then we created our first national constitution, the Articles of Confederation. A few years later we replaced the Articles with the Constitution we still have today. We are not the oldest country in the world, but our written Constitution has endured longer than that of any other people. That fact is worth not only celebrating, but pondering.

This is especially important for members of Congress. As these letters have had occasion to observe, Congress is at the very heart of our experiment in constitutional self-government. In the Constitution, Congress comes first: it is Article I. Congress holds the law-making power without which the president has much less to do and the federal courts nothing at all.

Congress also has the greatest responsibility for interpreting our Constitution. Most people think that it is the job of the Supreme Court to tell us what the Constitution means. It is true, as Alexander Hamilton wrote in *Federalist* 78, that "it is the proper and peculiar province of the courts to say what the law is," but many people have misinterpreted this passage. Hamilton does not say, and does not mean, that the Supreme Court is the only part of the federal government with the authority to interpret the Constitution, or that its interpretations are automatically supreme over Congress. He is simply defending the power of the federal courts to interpret the Constitution in order to decide the legal case in front of them, as courts must do. As he says in the essay, he is defending the independence of the federal courts, not their supremacy.

In fact, of all the branches, Congress has the primary authority to interpret the Constitution. Like the president or the Supreme Court, Congress receives its power from the Constitution. Just as the president has no authority to act against the Constitution, you in Congress have no authority to pass legislation that violates it. So – as the 112th Congress has distinguished itself by recognizing – every time you consider a bill, the first question you must ask yourself is not: "Do my constituents like it?" or even "Is it a good idea?" but "Is this constitutional?" That's not a matter of partisan politics; it's a matter of legitimate authority.

In asking the very question, "Is this bill constitutional?" members of Congress are interpreting the Constitution. You can take that duty seriously or unseriously, but you cannot avoid it. In making ordinary law, Congress necessarily makes a judgment on the meaning of the "Supreme Law of the Land." Unlike the other branches, however, Congress is the *first* place for these judgments. The president does not have to consider the constitutionality of a bill until it reaches his desk; the Supreme Court does not have to think about it unless and until a case reaches its bar. You must weigh it while the legislation is being drafted, while it is being examined in committee, and while it is being debated on the floor. A bill should never make it out of committee, much less Congress, without the most serious constitutional deliberation.

This is why it is so heartening that the 112th Congress began by reading the document that enumerates its powers, and why it is so important that bills cite their *constitutional* source of authority. It means that Congress is taking seriously its duty to interpret our Constitution.

In doing that, you are restoring an old tradition that had almost been forgotten. Since the beginning of the Republic, Congress has been *the* place for our nation's great constitutional debates. Consider the disputes in the 19th century over the national bank, or the tariff, or the power of Congress to prohibit slavery in the Western Territories. Or in the 20th century over regulating industry, establishing Social Security, or passing the War Powers Resolution. At each of these moments, it has been *Congress* that engaged in the most serious and searching debate on the meaning of the Constitution.

That constitutional deliberation must continue in Congress if we are going to restore the American experiment in self-government. For it is in Congress where the American people most fully govern themselves: where the common rights and responsibilities of the American people are submitted to law, and where the variety of the legitimate interests of the American people are most fully represented. When people's representatives engage in constitutional deliberation, the American people engage in it too.

This is a day to remember that if the Constitution is going to endure – if the American people are going to continue to be a constitutional people – Congress must be the place where the Constitution is most deeply studied, interpreted, and lived out. Only then will the habits and principles of constitutional government be restored in our law.

Happy Constitution Day.

OHIO FARMER

Appendices

Declaration of Independence

July 4, 1776

In Congress

The unanimous Declaration of the thirteen united States of America,

When in the Course of human events, it becomes necessary for one people to dissolve the political bands which have connected them with another, and to assume among the powers of the earth, the separate and equal station to which the Laws of Nature and of Nature's God entitle them, a decent respect to the opinions of mankind requires that they should declare the causes which impel them to the separation.

We hold these truths to be self-evident, that all men are created equal, that they are endowed by their Creator with certain unalienable Rights, that among these are Life, Liberty and the pursuit of Happiness. That to secure these rights, Governments are instituted among Men, deriving their just powers from the consent of the governed, that whenever any Form of Government becomes destructive of these ends, it is the Right of the People to alter or to abolish it, and to institute new Government, laying its foundation on such principles and organizing its powers in such form, as to them shall seem most likely to effect their Safety and Happiness. Prudence, indeed, will dictate that Governments long established should not be changed for light and transient causes; and accordingly all experience hath shewn, that mankind are more disposed to suffer, while evils are sufferable, than to right themselves by abolishing the forms to which they are accustomed. But when a long train of abuses and usurpations, pursuing invariably the same Object evinces a design to reduce them under absolute Despotism, it is their right, it is their duty, to throw off such Government, and to provide new Guards for their future security. Such has been the patient sufferance of these Colonies; and such is now the necessity which constrains them to alter their former Systems of Government. The history of the present King of Great Britain is a history of repeated injuries and usurpations, all having in direct object the establishment of an absolute Tyranny over these States. To prove this, let Facts be submitted to a candid world.

He has refused his Assent to Laws, the most wholesome and necessary for the public good.

He has forbidden his Governors to pass Laws of immediate and pressing importance, unless suspended in their operation till his Assent should be obtained; and when so suspended, he has utterly neglected to attend to them.

He has refused to pass other Laws for the accommodation of large districts of people, unless those people would relinquish the right of Representation in the Legislature, a right inestimable to them and formidable to tyrants only.

He has called together legislative bodies at places unusual, uncomfortable, and distant from the depository of their public Records, for the sole purpose of fatiguing them into compliance with his measures.

He has dissolved Representative Houses repeatedly, for opposing with manly firmness his invasions on the rights of the people.

He has refused for a long time, after such dissolutions, to cause others to be elected; whereby the Legislative powers, incapable of Annihilation, have returned to the People at large for their exercise; the State remaining in the mean time exposed to all the dangers of invasion from without, and convulsions within.

He has endeavoured to prevent the population of these States; for that purpose obstructing the Laws for Naturalization of Foreigners; refusing to pass others to encourage their migrations hither, and raising the conditions of new Appropriations of Lands.

He has obstructed the Administration of Justice, by refusing his Assent to Laws for establishing Judiciary powers.

He has made Judges dependent on his Will alone, for the tenure of their offices, and the amount and payment of their salaries.

He has erected a multitude of New Offices, and sent hither swarms of Officers to harrass our people, and eat out their substance.

He has kept among us, in times of peace, Standing Armies without the Consent of our legislatures.

He has affected to render the Military independent of and superior to the Civil power.

He has combined with others to subject us to a jurisdiction foreign to our constitution, and unacknowledged by our laws; giving his Assent to their Acts of pretended Legislation:

For Quartering large bodies of armed troops among us:

For protecting them, by a mock Trial, from punishment for any Murders which they should commit on the Inhabitants of these States:

For cutting off our Trade with all parts of the world:

For imposing Taxes on us without our Consent:

For depriving us in many cases, of the benefits of Trial by Jury:

For transporting us beyond Seas to be tried for pretended offences:

For abolishing the free System of English Laws in a neighbouring Province, establishing therein an Arbitrary government, and enlarging its Boundaries so as to render it at once an example and fit instrument for introducing the same absolute rule into these Colonies:

For taking away our Charters, abolishing our most valuable Laws, and altering fundamentally the Forms of our Governments:

For suspending our own Legislatures, and declaring themselves invested with power to legislate for us in all cases whatsoever.

He has abdicated Government here, by declaring us out of his Protection and waging War against us.

He has plundered our seas, ravaged our Coasts, burnt our towns, and destroyed the lives of our people.

He is at this time transporting large Armies of foreign Mercenaries to compleat the works of death, desolation and tyranny, already begun with circumstances of Cruelty & perfidy scarcely paralleled in the most barbarous ages, and totally unworthy the Head of a civilized nation.

He has constrained our fellow Citizens taken Captive on the high Seas to bear Arms against their Country, to become the executioners of their friends and Brethren, or to fall themselves by their Hands.

He has excited domestic insurrections amongst us, and has endeavoured to bring on the inhabitants of our frontiers, the merciless Indian Savages, whose known rule of warfare, is an undistinguished destruction of all ages, sexes and conditions.

In every stage of these Oppressions We have Petitioned for Redress in the most humble terms: Our repeated Petitions have been answered only by repeated injury. A Prince whose character is thus marked by every act which may define a Tyrant, is unfit to be the ruler of a free people.

Nor have We been wanting in attentions to our British brethren. We have warned them from time to time of attempts by their legislature to extend an unwarrantable jurisdiction over us. We have reminded them of the circumstances of our emigration and settlement here. We have appealed to their native justice and magnanimity, and we have conjured them by the ties of our common kindred to disavow these usurpations, which, would inevitably interrupt our connections and correspondence. They too have been deaf to the voice of justice and of consanguinity. We must, therefore, acquiesce in the necessity, which denounces our Separation, and hold them, as we hold the rest of mankind, Enemies in War, in Peace Friends.

We, therefore, the Representatives of the united States of America, in General Congress, Assembled, appealing to the Supreme Judge of the world for the rectitude of our intentions, do, in the Name, and by Authority of the good People of these Colonies, solemnly publish and declare, That these United Colonies are, and of Right ought to be Free and Independent States; that they are Absolved from all Allegiance to the British Crown, and that all political connection between them and the State of Great Britain, is and ought to be totally dissolved; and that as Free and Independent States, they have full Power to levy War, conclude Peace, contract Alliances, establish Commerce, and to do all other Acts and Things which Independent States may of right do. And for the support of this Declaration, with a firm reliance on the protection of divine Providence, we mutually pledge to each other our Lives, our Fortunes and our sacred Honor.

[Georgia:]
Button Gwinnett
Lyman Hall
George Walton

[North Carolina:]
William Hooper
Joseph Hewes
John Penn

[South Carolina:]
Edward Rutledge
Thomas Heyward, Jr.
Thomas Lynch, Jr.
Arthur Middleton

[Maryland:]
Samuel Chase
William Paca
Thomas Stone
Charles Carroll of Carrollton

[Virginia:]
George Wythe
Richard Henry Lee
Thomas Jefferson
Benjamin Harrison
Thomas Nelson, Jr.
Francis Lightfoot Lee
Carter Braxton

[Pennsylvania:]
Robert Morris
Benjamin Rush
Benjamin Franklin
John Morton
George Clymer
James Smith
George Taylor
James Wilson
George Ross

[Delaware:]
Caesar Rodney
George Read
Thomas McKean

[New York:]
William Floyd
Philip Livingston
Francis Lewis
Lewis Morris

[New Jersey:]
Richard Stockton
John Witherspoon
Francis Hopkinson
John Hart
Abraham Clark

[New Hampshire:]
Josiah Bartlett
William Whipple
Matthew Thornton

[Massachusetts:]
John Hancock
Samuel Adams
John Adams
Robert Treat Paine
Elbridge Gerry

[Rhode Island:]
Stephen Hopkins
William Ellery

[Connecticut:]
Roger Sherman
Samuel Huntington
William Williams
Oliver Wolcott

Constitution of the United States

1787

We the People of the United States, in Order to form a more perfect Union, establish Justice, insure domestic Tranquility, provide for the common defence, promote the general Welfare, and secure the Blessings of Liberty to ourselves and our Posterity, do ordain and establish this Constitution for the United States of America.

Article. I.

Section. 1. All legislative Powers herein granted shall be vested in a Congress of the United States, which shall consist of a Senate and House of Representatives.

Section. 2. The House of Representatives shall be composed of Members chosen every second Year by the People of the several States, and the Electors in each State shall have the Qualifications requisite for Electors of the most numerous Branch of the State Legislature.

No Person shall be a Representative who shall not have attained to the Age of twenty five Years, and been seven Years a Citizen of the United States, and who shall not, when elected, be an Inhabitant of that State in which he shall be chosen.

[Representatives and direct Taxes shall be apportioned among the several States which may be included within this Union, according to their respective Numbers, which shall be determined by adding to the whole Number of free Persons, including those bound to Service for a Term of Years, and excluding Indians not taxed, three fifths of all other Persons.]* The actual Enumeration shall be made within three Years after the first Meeting of the Congress of the United States, and within every subsequent Term of ten Years, in such Manner as they shall by Law direct. The Number of Representatives shall not exceed one for every thirty Thousand, but each State shall have at Least one Representative; and until

---

* Changed by Section 2 of the Fourteenth Amendment.

such enumeration shall be made, the State of New Hampshire shall be entitled to chuse three, Massachusetts eight, Rhode-Island and Providence Plantations one, Connecticut five, New-York six, New Jersey four, Pennsylvania eight, Delaware one, Maryland six, Virginia ten, North Carolina five, South Carolina five, and Georgia three.

When vacancies happen in the Representation from any State, the Executive Authority thereof shall issue Writs of Election to fill such Vacancies.

The House of Representatives shall chuse their Speaker and other Officers; and shall have the sole Power of Impeachment.

Section. 3. The Senate of the United States shall be composed of two Senators from each State, [chosen by the Legislature thereof,]* for six Years; and each Senator shall have one Vote.

Immediately after they shall be assembled in Consequence of the first Election, they shall be divided as equally as may be into three Classes. The Seats of the Senators of the first Class shall be vacated at the Expiration of the second Year, of the second Class at the Expiration of the fourth Year, and of the third Class at the Expiration of the sixth Year, so that one third may be chosen every second Year; [and if Vacancies happen by Resignation, or otherwise, during the Recess of the Legislature of any State, the Executive thereof may make temporary Appointments until the next Meeting of the Legislature, which shall then fill such Vacancies.]†

No Person shall be a Senator who shall not have attained to the Age of thirty Years, and been nine Years a Citizen of the United States, and who shall not, when elected, be an Inhabitant of that State for which he shall be chosen.

The Vice President of the United States shall be President of the Senate, but shall have no Vote, unless they be equally divided.

The Senate shall chuse their other Officers, and also a President pro tempore, in the Absence of the Vice President, or when he shall exercise the Office of President of the United States.

The Senate shall have the sole Power to try all Impeachments. When sitting for that Purpose, they shall be on Oath or Affirmation. When the President of the United States is tried, the Chief Justice shall preside: And

---

* Changed by the Seventeenth Amendment.
† Changed by the Seventeenth Amendment.

no Person shall be convicted without the Concurrence of two thirds of the Members present.

Judgment in Cases of Impeachment shall not extend further than to removal from Office, and disqualification to hold and enjoy any Office of honor, Trust or Profit under the United States: but the Party convicted shall nevertheless be liable and subject to Indictment, Trial, Judgment and Punishment, according to Law.

Section. 4. The Times, Places and Manner of holding Elections for Senators and Representatives, shall be prescribed in each State by the Legislature thereof; but the Congress may at any time by Law make or alter such Regulations, except as to the Places of chusing Senators.

The Congress shall assemble at least once in every Year, and such Meeting shall be [on the first Monday in December,]* unless they shall by Law appoint a different Day.

Section. 5. Each House shall be the Judge of the Elections, Returns and Qualifications of its own Members, and a Majority of each shall constitute a Quorum to do Business; but a smaller Number may adjourn from day to day, and may be authorized to compel the Attendance of absent Members, in such Manner, and under such Penalties as each House may provide.

Each House may determine the Rules of its Proceedings, punish its Members for disorderly Behaviour, and, with the Concurrence of two thirds, expel a Member.

Each House shall keep a Journal of its Proceedings, and from time to time publish the same, excepting such Parts as may in their Judgment require Secrecy; and the Yeas and Nays of the Members of either House on any question shall, at the Desire of one fifth of those Present, be entered on the Journal.

Neither House, during the Session of Congress, shall, without the Consent of the other, adjourn for more than three days, nor to any other Place than that in which the two Houses shall be sitting.

Section. 6. The Senators and Representatives shall receive a Compensation for their Services, to be ascertained by Law, and paid out of the Treasury of the United States. They shall in all Cases, except Treason, Felony and Breach of the Peace, be privileged from Arrest during their

---

* Changed by Section 2 of the Twentieth Amendment.

Attendance at the Session of their respective Houses, and in going to and returning from the same; and for any Speech or Debate in either House, they shall not be questioned in any other Place.

No Senator or Representative shall, during the Time for which he was elected, be appointed to any civil Office under the Authority of the United States, which shall have been created, or the Emoluments whereof shall have been encreased during such time; and no Person holding any Office under the United States, shall be a Member of either House during his Continuance in Office.

Section. 7. All Bills for raising Revenue shall originate in the House of Representatives; but the Senate may propose or concur with Amendments as on other Bills.

Every Bill which shall have passed the House of Representatives and the Senate, shall, before it become a Law, be presented to the President of the United States; If he approve he shall sign it, but if not he shall return it, with his Objections to that House in which it shall have originated, who shall enter the Objections at large on their Journal, and proceed to reconsider it. If after such Reconsideration two thirds of that House shall agree to pass the Bill, it shall be sent, together with the Objections, to the other House, by which it shall likewise be reconsidered, and if approved by two thirds of that House, it shall become a Law. But in all such Cases the Votes of both Houses shall be determined by yeas and Nays, and the Names of the Persons voting for and against the Bill shall be entered on the Journal of each House respectively. If any Bill shall not be returned by the President within ten Days (Sundays excepted) after it shall have been presented to him, the Same shall be a Law, in like Manner as if he had signed it, unless the Congress by their Adjournment prevent its Return, in which Case it shall not be a Law.

Every Order, Resolution, or Vote to which the Concurrence of the Senate and House of Representatives may be necessary (except on a question of Adjournment) shall be presented to the President of the United States; and before the Same shall take Effect, shall be approved by him, or being disapproved by him, shall be repassed by two thirds of the Senate and House of Representatives, according to the Rules and Limitations prescribed in the Case of a Bill.

Section. 8. The Congress shall have Power To lay and collect Taxes, Duties, Imposts and Excises, to pay the Debts and provide for the common Defence and general Welfare of the United States; but all Duties, Imposts and Excises shall be uniform throughout the United States;

To borrow Money on the credit of the United States;

To regulate Commerce with foreign Nations, and among the several States, and with the Indian Tribes;

To establish an uniform Rule of Naturalization, and uniform Laws on the subject of Bankruptcies throughout the United States;

To coin Money, regulate the Value thereof, and of foreign Coin, and fix the Standard of Weights and Measures;

To provide for the Punishment of counterfeiting the Securities and current Coin of the United States;

To establish Post Offices and post Roads;

To promote the Progress of Science and useful Arts, by securing for limited Times to Authors and Inventors the exclusive Right to their respective Writings and Discoveries;

To constitute Tribunals inferior to the supreme Court;

To define and punish Piracies and Felonies committed on the high Seas, and Offenses against the Law of Nations;

To declare War, grant Letters of Marque and Reprisal, and make Rules concerning Captures on Land and Water;

To raise and support Armies, but no Appropriation of Money to that Use shall be for a longer Term than two Years;

To provide and maintain a Navy;

To make Rules for the Government and Regulation of the land and naval Forces;

To provide for calling forth the Militia to execute the Laws of the Union, suppress Insurrections and repel Invasions;

To provide for organizing, arming, and disciplining, the Militia, and for governing such Part of them as may be employed in the Service of the United States, reserving to the States respectively, the Appointment of the Officers, and the Authority of training the Militia according to the discipline prescribed by Congress;

To exercise exclusive Legislation in all Cases whatsoever, over such District (not exceeding ten Miles square) as may, by Cession of particular States, and the Acceptance of Congress, become the Seat of the Government of the United States, and to exercise like Authority over all Places purchased by the Consent of the Legislature of the State in which the Same shall be, for the Erection of Forts, Magazines, Arsenals, dock-Yards, and other needful Buildings; – And

To make all Laws which shall be necessary and proper for carrying into Execution the foregoing Powers, and all other Powers vested by this Constitution in the Government of the United States, or in any Department or Officer thereof.

Section. 9. The Migration or Importation of such Persons as any of the States now existing shall think proper to admit, shall not be prohibited by the Congress prior to the Year one thousand eight hundred and eight, but a Tax or duty may be imposed on such Importation, not exceeding ten dollars for each Person.

The Privilege of the Writ of Habeas Corpus shall not be suspended, unless when in Cases of Rebellion or Invasion the public Safety may require it.

No Bill of Attainder or ex post facto Law shall be passed.

No Capitation, or other direct, Tax shall be laid, unless in Proportion to the Census or Enumeration herein before directed to be taken.*

No Tax or Duty shall be laid on Articles exported from any State.

No Preference shall be given by any Regulation of Commerce or Revenue to the Ports of one State over those of another: nor shall Vessels bound to, or from, one State, be obliged to enter, clear, or pay Duties in another.

No Money shall be drawn from the Treasury, but in Consequence of Appropriations made by Law; and a regular Statement and Account of the Receipts and Expenditures of all public Money shall be published from time to time.

No Title of Nobility shall be granted by the United States: And no Person holding any Office of Profit or Trust under them, shall, without the Consent of the Congress, accept of any present, Emolument, Office, or Title, of any kind whatever, from any King, Prince, or foreign State.

Section. 10. No State shall enter into any Treaty, Alliance, or Confederation; grant Letters of Marque and Reprisal; coin Money; emit Bills of Credit; make any Thing but gold and silver Coin a Tender in Payment of Debts; pass any Bill of Attainder, ex post facto Law, or Law impairing the Obligation of Contracts, or grant any Title of Nobility.

---

* See Sixteenth Amendment.

No State shall, without the Consent of the Congress, lay any Imposts or Duties on Imports or Exports, except what may be absolutely necessary for executing it's inspection Laws: and the net Produce of all Duties and Imposts, laid by any State on Imports or Exports, shall be for the Use of the Treasury of the United States; and all such Laws shall be subject to the Revision and Controul of the Congress.

No State shall, without the Consent of Congress, lay any Duty of Tonnage, keep Troops, or Ships of War in time of Peace, enter into any Agreement or Compact with another State, or with a foreign Power, or engage in War, unless actually invaded, or in such imminent Danger as will not admit of delay.

Article. II.

Section. 1. The executive Power shall be vested in a President of the United States of America. He shall hold his Office during the Term of four Years, and, together with the Vice President, chosen for the same Term, be elected, as follows:

Each State shall appoint, in such Manner as the Legislature thereof may direct, a Number of Electors, equal to the whole Number of Senators and Representatives to which the State may be entitled in the Congress: but no Senator or Representative, or Person holding an Office of Trust or Profit under the United States, shall be appointed an Elector.

[The Electors shall meet in their respective States, and vote by Ballot for two Persons, of whom one at least shall not be an Inhabitant of the same State with themselves. And they shall make a List of all the Persons voted for, and of the Number of Votes for each; which List they shall sign and certify, and transmit sealed to the Seat of the Government of the United States, directed to the President of the Senate. The President of the Senate shall, in the Presence of the Senate and House of Representatives, open all the Certificates, and the Votes shall then be counted. The Person having the greatest Number of Votes shall be the President, if such Number be a Majority of the whole Number of Electors appointed; and if there be more than one who have such Majority, and have an equal Number of Votes, then the House of Representatives shall immediately chuse by Ballot one of them for President; and if no Person have a Majority, then from the five highest on the List the said House shall in like Manner chuse the President. But in chusing the President, the

Votes shall be taken by States, the Representation from each State having one Vote; A quorum for this purpose shall consist of a Member or Members from two thirds of the States, and a Majority of all the States shall be necessary to a Choice. In every Case, after the Choice of the President, the Person having the greatest Number of Votes of the Electors shall be the Vice President. But if there should remain two or more who have equal Votes, the Senate shall chuse from them by Ballot the Vice President.]*

The Congress may determine the Time of chusing the Electors, and the Day on which they shall give their Votes; which Day shall be the same throughout the United States.

No Persons except a natural born Citizen, or a Citizen of the United States, at the time of the Adoption of this Constitution, shall be eligible to the Office of President; neither shall any Person be eligible to that Office who shall not have attained to the Age of thirty five Years, and been fourteen Years a Resident within the United States.

[In Case of the Removal of the President from Office, or of his Death, Resignation, or Inability to discharge the Powers and Duties of the said Office, the Same shall devolve on the Vice President, and the Congress may by Law provide for the Case of Removal, Death, Resignation or Inability, both of the President and Vice President, declaring what Officer shall then act as President, and such Officer shall act accordingly, until the Disability be removed, or a President shall be elected.]†

The President shall, at stated Times, receive for his Services, a Compensation, which shall neither be increased nor diminished during the Period for which he shall have been elected, and he shall not receive within that Period any other Emolument from the United States, or any of them.

Before he enter on the Execution of his Office, he shall take the following Oath or Affirmation: – "I do solemnly swear (or affirm) that I will faithfully execute the Office of President of the United States, and will to the best of my Ability, preserve, protect and defend the Constitution of the United States."

---

* Changed by the Twelfth Amendment.
† Changed by the Twenty-Fifth Amendment.

Section. 2. The President shall be Commander in Chief of the Army and Navy of the United States, and of the Militia of the several States, when called into the actual Service of the United States; he may require the Opinion, in writing, of the principal Officer in each of the executive Departments, upon any Subject relating to the Duties of their respective Offices, and he shall have Power to grant Reprieves and Pardons for Offences against the United States, except in Cases of Impeachment.

He shall have Power, by and with the Advice and Consent of the Senate, to make Treaties, provided two thirds of the Senators present concur; and he shall nominate, and by and with the Advice and Consent of the Senate, shall appoint Ambassadors, other public Ministers and Consuls, Judges of the supreme Court, and all other Officers of the United States, whose Appointments are not herein otherwise provided for, and which shall be established by Law: but the Congress may by Law vest the Appointment of such inferior Officers, as they think proper, in the President alone, in the Courts of Law, or in the Heads of Departments.

The President shall have Power to fill up all Vacancies that may happen during the Recess of the Senate, by granting Commissions which shall expire at the End of their next Session.

Section. 3. He shall from time to time give to the Congress Information of the State of the Union, and recommend to their Consideration such Measures as he shall judge necessary and expedient; he may, on extraordinary Occasions, convene both Houses, or either of them, and in Case of Disagreement between them, with Respect to the Time of Adjournment, he may adjourn them to such Time as he shall think proper; he shall receive Ambassadors and other public Ministers; he shall take Care that the Laws be faithfully executed, and shall Commission all the Officers of the United States.

Section. 4. The President, Vice President and all civil Officers of the United States, shall be removed from Office on Impeachment for, and Conviction of, Treason, Bribery, or other high Crimes and Misdemeanors.

Article. III.

Section. 1. The judicial Power of the United States, shall be vested in one supreme Court, and in such inferior Courts as the Congress may from time to time ordain and establish. The Judges, both of the supreme and inferior Courts, shall hold their Offices during good Behaviour, and shall, at stated Times, receive for their Services, a Compensation, which shall not be diminished during their Continuance in Office.

Section. 2. The judicial Power shall extend to all Cases, in Law and Equity, arising under this Constitution, the Laws of the United States, and Treaties made, or which shall be made, under their Authority; – to all Cases affecting Ambassadors, other public Ministers and Consuls; – to all Cases of admiralty and maritime Jurisdiction; – to Controversies to which the United States shall be a Party; – to Controversies between two or more States; – [between a State and Citizens of another State; –]* between Citizens of different States; – between Citizens of the same State claiming Lands under Grants of different States, [and between a State, or the Citizens thereof, and foreign States, Citizens or Subjects.]†

In all Cases affecting Ambassadors, other public Ministers and Consuls, and those in which a State shall be Party, the supreme Court shall have original Jurisdiction. In all the other Cases before mentioned, the supreme Court shall have appellate Jurisdiction, both as to Law and Fact, with such Exceptions, and under such Regulations as the Congress shall make. The Trial of all Crimes, except in Cases of Impeachment, shall be by Jury; and such Trial shall be held in the State where the said Crimes shall have been committed; but when not committed within any State, the Trial shall be at such Place or Places as the Congress may by Law have directed.

Section. 3. Treason against the United States, shall consist only in levying War against them, or in adhering to their Enemies, giving them Aid and Comfort. No Person shall be convicted of Treason unless on the Testimony of two Witnesses to the same overt Act, or on Confession in open Court.

The Congress shall have Power to declare the Punishment of Treason, but no Attainder of Treason shall work Corruption of Blood, or Forfeiture except during the Life of the Person attained.

Article. IV.

Section. 1. Full Faith and Credit shall be given in each State to the public Acts, Records, and judicial Proceedings of every other State. And

---

* Changed by the Eleventh Amendment.
† Changed by the Eleventh Amendment.

the Congress may by general Laws prescribe the Manner in which such Acts, Records and Proceedings shall be proved, and the Effect thereof.

Section. 2. The Citizens of each State shall be entitled to all Privileges and Immunities of Citizens in the several States.

A Person charged in any State with Treason, Felony, or other Crime, who shall flee from Justice, and be found in another State, shall on Demand of the executive Authority of the State from which he fled, be delivered up, to be removed to the State having Jurisdiction of the Crime.

[No Person held to Service or Labour in one State, under the Laws thereof, escaping into another, shall, in Consequence of any Law or Regulation therein, be discharged from such Service or Labour, but shall be delivered up on Claim of the Party to whom such Service or Labour may be due.]*

Section. 3. New States may be admitted by the Congress into this Union; but no new State shall be formed or erected within the Jurisdiction of any other State; nor any State be formed by the Junction of two or more States, or Parts of States, without the Consent of the Legislatures of the States concerned as well as of the Congress.

The Congress shall have Power to dispose of and make all needful Rules and Regulations respecting the Territory or other Property belonging to the United States; and nothing in this Constitution shall be so construed as to Prejudice any Claims of the United States, or of any particular State.

Section. 4. The United States shall guarantee to every State in this Union a Republican Form of Government, and shall protect each of them against Invasion; and on Application of the Legislature, or of the Executive (when the Legislature cannot be convened) against domestic Violence.

Article. V.

The Congress, whenever two thirds of both Houses shall deem it necessary, shall propose Amendments to this Constitution, or, on the Application of the Legislatures of two thirds of the several States, shall call a Convention for proposing Amendments, which, in either Case, shall be valid to all Intents and Purposes, as Part of this Constitution, when ratified by the Legislatures of three fourths of the several States, or by

---

* Changed by the Thirteenth Amendment.

Conventions in three fourths thereof, as the one or the other Mode of Ratification may be proposed by the Congress; Provided that no Amendment which may be made prior to the Year One thousand eight hundred and eight shall in any Manner affect the first and fourth Clauses in the Ninth Section of the first Article; and that no State, without its Consent, shall be deprived of its equal Suffrage in the Senate.

Article. VI.

All Debts contracted and Engagements entered into, before the Adoption of this Constitution, shall be as valid against the United States under this Constitution, as under the Confederation.

This Constitution, and the Laws of the United States which shall be made in Pursuance thereof; and all Treaties made, or which shall be made, under the Authority of the United States, shall be the supreme Law of the Land; and the Judges in every State shall be bound thereby, any Thing in the Constitution or Laws of any State to the Contrary notwithstanding.

The Senators and Representatives before mentioned, and the Members of the several State Legislatures, and all executive and judicial Officers, both of the United States and of the several States, shall be bound by Oath or Affirmation, to support this Constitution; but no religious Test shall ever be required as a Qualification to any Office or public Trust under the United States.

Article. VII.

The Ratification of the Conventions of nine States, shall be sufficient for the Establishment of this Constitution between the States so ratifying the Same.

Done in Convention by the Unanimous Consent of the States present the Seventeenth Day of September in the Year of our Lord one thousand seven hundred and Eighty seven and of the Independence of the United States of America the Twelfth In Witness whereof We have hereunto subscribed our Names,

Go. Washington – Presidt. and
deputy from Virginia

[New Hampshire:]
John Langdon
Nicholas Gilman

[Massachusetts:]
Nathaniel Gorham
Rufus King

[Connecticut:]
Wm. Saml. Johnson
Roger Sherman

[New York:]
Alexander Hamilton

[New Jersey:]
Wil: Livingston
David Brearley
Wm. Paterson
Jona: Dayton

[Pennsylvania:]
B Franklin
Thomas Mifflin
Robt. Morris
Geo. Clymer
Thos. FitzSimons
Jared Ingersoll
James Wilson
Gouv Morris

[Delaware:]
Geo: Read
Gunning Bedford jun
John Dickinson
Richard Bassett
Jaco: Broom

[Maryland:]
James McHenry
Dan of St Thos. Jenifer
Danl. Carroll

[Virginia:]
John Blair –
James Madison Jr.

[North Carolina:]
Wm. Blount
Richd. Dobbs Spaight
Hu Williamson

[South Carolina:]
J. Rutledge
Charles Cotesworth Pinckney
Charles Pinckney
Pierce Butler

[Georgia:]
William Few
Abr Baldwin

Attest William Jackson
Secretary

Amendment I.

Ratified December 15, 1791

Congress shall make no law respecting an establishment of religion, or prohibiting the free exercise thereof; or abridging the freedom of speech, or of the press; or the right of the people peaceably to assemble, and to petition the Government for a redress of grievances.

Amendment II.

Ratified December 15, 1791

A well regulated Militia, being necessary to the security of a free State, the right of the people to keep and bear Arms, shall not be infringed.

Amendment III.

Ratified December 15, 1791

No Soldier shall, in time of peace be quartered in any house, without the consent of the Owner, nor in time of war, but in a manner to be prescribed by law.

Amendment IV.

Ratified December 15, 1791

The right of the people to be secure in their persons, houses, papers, and effects, against unreasonable searches and seizures, shall not be violated, and no Warrants shall issue, but upon probable cause, supported by Oath or affirmation, and particularly describing the place to be searched, and the persons or things to be seized.

Amendment V.

Ratified December 15, 1791

No person shall be held to answer for a capital, or otherwise infamous crime, unless on a presentment or indictment of a Grand Jury, except in cases arising in the land or naval forces, or in the Militia, when in actual service in time of War or public danger; nor shall any person be subject for the same offence to be twice put in jeopardy of life or limb, nor shall be compelled in any criminal case to be a witness against himself, nor be deprived of life, liberty, or property, without due process of law; nor shall private property be taken for public use, without just compensation.

Amendment VI.

Ratified December 15, 1791

In all criminal prosecutions, the accused shall enjoy the right to a speedy and public trial, by an impartial jury of the State and district wherein the crime shall have been committed, which district shall have been previously ascertained by law, and to be informed of the nature and cause of the accusation; to be confronted with the witnesses against him; to have compulsory process for obtaining witnesses in his favor, and to have the assistance of counsel for his defence.

Amendment VII.

Ratified December 15, 1791

In Suits at common law, where the value in controversy shall exceed twenty dollars, the right of trial by jury shall be preserved, and no fact tried by a jury, shall be otherwise reexamined in any Court of the United States, than according to the rules of the common law.

Amendment VIII.

Ratified December 15, 1791

Excessive bail shall not be required, nor excessive fines imposed, nor cruel and unusual punishments inflicted.

Amendment IX.

Ratified December 15, 1791

The enumeration in the Constitution, of certain rights, shall not be construed to deny or disparage others retained by the people.

Amendment X.

Ratified December 15, 1791

The powers not delegated to the United States by the Constitution, nor prohibited by it to the States, are reserved to the States respectively, or to the people.

Amendment XI.

Ratified February 7, 1795

The Judicial power of the United States shall not be construed to extend to any suit in law or equity, commenced or prosecuted against one of the United States by Citizens of another State, or by Citizens or Subjects of any Foreign State.

Amendment XII.

Ratified June 15, 1804

The Electors shall meet in their respective states, and vote by ballot for President and Vice President, one of whom, at least, shall not be an inhabitant of the same state with themselves; they shall name in their ballots the person voted for as President, and in distinct ballots the person voted for as Vice-President, and they shall make distinct lists of all persons voted for as President, and of all persons voted for as Vice-President, and of the number of votes for each, which lists they shall sign and certify, and transmit sealed to the seat of the government of the United States, directed to the President of the Senate; – The President of the Senate shall, in the presence of the Senate and House of Representatives, open all the certificates and the votes shall then be counted; – The person having the greatest number of votes for President, shall be the President, if such number be a majority of the whole number of Electors appointed; and if no person have such majority, then from the persons having the highest numbers not exceeding three on the list of those voted for as President, the House of Representatives shall choose immediately, by ballot, the President. But in choosing the President, the votes shall be taken by states, the representation from each state having one vote; a quorum for this purpose shall consist of a member or members from two-thirds of the states, and a majority of all the states shall be necessary to a choice. [And if the House of Representatives shall not choose a President whenever the right of choice shall devolve upon them, before the fourth day of March next following, then the Vice-President shall act as President, as in the case of the death or other constitutional disability of the President.* The person having the greatest number of votes as Vice-President, shall be the Vice-President, if such number be a majority of the whole number of Electors appointed, and if no person have a majority, then from the two highest numbers on the list, the Senate shall choose the Vice-President; a quorum for the purpose shall consist of two-thirds of the whole number of Senators, and a majority of the whole number shall be necessary to a choice. But no person constitutionally ineligible to the office of President shall be eligible to that of Vice-President of the United States.

Amendment XIII.

Ratified December 6, 1865

Section 1. Neither slavery nor involuntary servitude, except as a punishment for crime whereof the party shall have been duly convicted, shall exist within the United States, or any place subject to their jurisdiction.

Section 2. Congress shall have the power to enforce this article by appropriate legislation.

Amendment XIV.

Ratified July 9, 1868

Section 1. All persons born or naturalized in the United States, and subject to the jurisdiction thereof, are citizens of the United States and of the State wherein they reside. No State shall make or enforce any law which shall abridge the privileges or immunities of citizens of the United States; nor shall any State deprive any person of life, liberty, or property, without due process of law; nor deny to any person within its jurisdiction the equal protection of the laws.

---

* Superseded by Section 3 of the Twentieth Amendment.

Section 2. Representatives shall be apportioned among the several States according to their respective numbers, counting the whole number of persons in each State, excluding Indians not taxed. But when the right to vote at any election for the choice of electors for President and Vice President of the United States, Representatives in Congress, the Executive and Judicial officers of a State, or the members of the Legislature thereof, is denied to any of the male inhabitants of such State, being twenty-one years of age,* and citizens of the United States, or in any way abridged, except for participation in rebellion, or other crime, the basis of representation therein shall be reduced in the proportion which the number of such male citizens shall bear to the whole number of male citizens twenty-one years of age in such State.

Section 3. No person shall be a Senator or Representative in Congress, or elector of President and Vice President, or hold any office, civil or military, under the United States, or under any State, who, having previously taken an oath, as a member of Congress, or as an officer of the United States, or as a member of any State legislature, or as an executive or judicial officer of any State, to support the Constitution of the United States, shall have engaged in insurrection or rebellion against the same, or given aid or comfort to the enemies thereof. But Congress may by a vote of two-thirds of each House, remove such disability.

Section 4. The validity of the public debt of the United States, authorized by law, including debts incurred for payment of pensions and bounties for services in suppressing insurrection or rebellion, shall not be questioned. But neither the United States nor any State shall assume or pay any debt or obligation incurred in aid of insurrection or rebellion against the United States, or any claim for the loss or emancipation of any slave; but all such debts, obligations and claims shall be held illegal and void.

Section 5. The Congress shall have power to enforce, by appropriate legislation, the provisions of this article.

---

* Changed by Section 1 of the Twenty-Sixth Amendment.

Amendment XV.

Ratified February 3, 1870

Section 1. The right of citizens of the United States to vote shall not be denied or abridged by the United States or by any State on account of race, color, or previous condition of servitude.

Section 2. The Congress shall have power to enforce this article by appropriate legislation.

Amendment XVI.

Ratified February 3, 1913

The Congress shall have power to lay and collect taxes on incomes, from whatever source derived, without apportionment among the several States, and without regard to any census or enumeration.

Amendment XVII.

Ratified April 8, 1913

The Senate of the United States shall be composed of two Senators from each State, elected by the people thereof, for six years; and each Senator shall have one vote. The electors in each State shall have the qualifications requisite for electors of the most numerous branch of the State legislatures.

When vacancies happen in the representation of any State in the Senate, the executive authority of such State shall issue writs of election to fill such vacancies: Provided, That the legislature of any State may empower the executive thereof to make temporary appointments until the people fill the vacancies by election as the legislature may direct.

This amendment shall not be so construed as to affect the election or term of any Senator chosen before it becomes valid as part of the Constitution.

Amendment XVIII.

Ratified January 16, 1919

Section 1. After one year from the ratification of this article the manufacture, sale, or transportation of intoxicating liquors within, the importation thereof into, or the exportation thereof from the United States and all territory subject to the jurisdiction thereof for beverage purposes is hereby prohibited.

Section 2. The Congress and the several States shall have concurrent power to enforce this article by appropriate legislation.

Section 3. This article shall be inoperative unless it shall have been ratified as an amendment to the Constitution by the legislatures of the several States, as provided in the Constitution, within seven years from the date of the submission hereof to the States by the Congress*

Amendment XIX.

Ratified August 18, 1920

The right of citizens of the United States to vote shall not be denied or abridged by the United States or by any State on account of sex.

Congress shall have power to enforce this article by appropriate legislation.

Amendment XX.

Ratified January 23, 1933

Section 1. The terms of the President and Vice President shall end at noon on the 20th day of January, and the terms of Senators and Representatives at noon on the 3d day of January, of the years in which such terms would have ended if this article had not been ratified; and the terms of their successors shall then begin.

Section 2. The Congress shall assemble at least once in every year, and such meeting shall begin at noon on the 3d day of January, unless they shall by law appoint a different day.

---

* Repealed by the Twenty-First Amendment.

Section 3. If, at the time fixed for the beginning of the term of the President, the President elect shall have died, the Vice President elect shall become President. If a President shall not have been chosen before the time fixed for the beginning of his term, or if the President elect shall have failed to qualify, then the Vice President elect shall act as President until a President shall have qualified; and the Congress may by law provide for the case wherein neither a President elect nor a Vice President elect shall have qualified, declaring who shall then act as President, or the manner in which one who is to act shall be selected, and such person shall act accordingly until a President or Vice President shall have qualified.

Section 4. The Congress may by law provide for the case of the death of any of the persons from whom the House of Representatives may choose a President whenever the right of choice shall have devolved upon them, and for the case of the death of any of the persons from whom the Senate may choose a Vice President whenever the right of choice shall have devolved upon them.

Section 5. Sections 1 and 2 shall take effect on the 15th day of October following the ratification of this article.

Section 6. This article shall be inoperative unless it shall have been ratified as an amendment to the Constitution by the legislatures of three-fourths of the several States within seven years from the date of its submission.

Amendment XXI.

Ratified December 5, 1933

Section 1. The eighteenth article of amendment to the Constitution of the United States is hereby repealed.

Section 2. The transportation or importation into any State, Territory, or possession of the United States for delivery or use therein of intoxicating liquors, in violation of the laws thereof, is hereby prohibited.

Section 3. This article shall be inoperative unless it shall have been ratified as an amendment to the Constitution by conventions in the several States, as provided in the Constitution, within seven years from the date of the submission hereof to the States by the Congress.

Amendment XXII.

Ratified February 27, 1951

Section 1. No person shall be elected to the office of the President more than twice, and no person who has held the office of President, or acted as President, for more than two years of a term to which some other person was elected President shall be elected to the office of the President more than once. But this Article shall not apply to any person holding the office of President when this Article was proposed by the Congress, and shall not prevent any person who may be holding the office of President, or acting as President, during the term within which this Article becomes operative from holding the office of President or acting as President during the remainder of such term.

Section 2. This article shall be inoperative unless it shall have been ratified as an amendment to the Constitution by the legislatures of three-fourths of the several States within seven years from the date of its submission to the States by the Congress.

Amendment XXIII.

Ratified March 29, 1961

Section 1. The District constituting the seat of Government of the United States shall appoint in such manner as the Congress may direct:

A number of electors of President and Vice President equal to the whole number of Senators and Representatives in Congress to which the District would be entitled if it were a State, but in no event more than the least populous State; they shall be in addition to those appointed by the States, but they shall be considered, for the purposes of the election of President and Vice President, to be electors appointed by a State; and they shall meet in the District and perform such duties as provided by the twelfth article of amendment.

Section 2. The Congress shall have power to enforce this article by appropriate legislation.

Amendment XXIV.

Ratified January 23, 1964

Section 1. The right of citizens of the United States to vote in any primary or other election for President or Vice President, for electors for President or Vice President, or for Senator or Representative in Congress, shall not be denied or abridged by the United States or any State by reason of failure to pay any poll tax or other tax.

Section 2. The Congress shall have the power to enforce this article by appropriate legislation.

Amendment XXV.

Ratified February 10, 1967

Section 1. In case of the removal of the President from office or of his death or resignation, the Vice President shall become President.

Section 2. Whenever there is a vacancy in the office of the Vice President, the President shall nominate a Vice President who shall take office upon confirmation by a majority vote of both Houses of Congress.

Section 3. Whenever the President transmits to the President pro tempore of the Senate and the Speaker of the House of Representatives his written declaration that he is unable to discharge the powers and duties of his office, and until he transmits to them a written declaration to the contrary, such powers and duties shall be discharged by the Vice President as Acting President.

Section 4. Whenever the Vice President and a majority of either the principal officers of the executive departments or of such other body as Congress may by law provide, transmit to the President pro tempore of the Senate and the Speaker of the House of Representatives their written declaration that the President is unable to discharge the powers and duties of his office, the Vice President shall immediately assume the powers and duties of the office as Acting President.

Thereafter, when the President transmits to the President pro tempore of the Senate and the Speaker of the House of Representatives his written declaration that no inability exists, he shall resume the powers and duties of his office unless the Vice President and a majority of either the principal officers of the executive department or of such other body as

Congress may by law provide, transmit within four days to the President pro tempore of the Senate and the Speaker of the House of Representatives their written declaration that the President is unable to discharge the powers and duties of his office. Thereupon Congress shall decide the issue, assembling within forty-eight hours for that purpose if not in session. If the Congress, within twenty-one days after receipt of the latter written declaration, or, if Congress is not in session, within twenty-one days after Congress is required to assemble, determines by two-thirds vote of both Houses that the President is unable to discharge the powers and duties of his office, the Vice President shall continue to discharge the same as Acting President; otherwise, the President shall resume the powers and duties of his office.

Amendment XXVI.

Ratified July 1, 1971

Section 1. The right of citizens of the United States, who are eighteen years of age or older, to vote shall not be denied or abridged by the United States or by any State on account of age.

Section 2. The Congress shall have power to enforce this article by appropriate legislation.

Amendment XXVII.

Ratified May 7, 1992

No law varying the compensation for the services of the Senators and Representatives shall take effect, until an election of Representatives shall have intervened.

Index

Ashbrook Center at Ashland University

The Ashbrook Center, located on the campus of Ashland University, seeks to restore and strengthen the capacities of the American people for constitutional self-government. Through undergraduate, graduate, and civic programs, the Ashbrook Center is the nation's largest university based educator in the enduring principles and practice of free government in the United States. Dedicated in 1983 by President Ronald Reagan, the Ashbrook Center is an independent center governed by its own board and responsible for raising all of the funds necessary for its many programs.

The Ashbrook Center transforms the lives of students by inviting them into a true liberal education – an education for freedom. Ashbrook Scholars join one another as friends, studying the best that has been thought and done in the hope of understanding what is good and noble and just. From their Ashbrook education, our students learn why America is worthy of their study and love, and they become better equipped to take a leading role in their country's civic life.

The Ashbrook Center also offers teachers the opportunity to study with some of the best history and government scholars in the country. Bringing together teachers and scholars from across America, the Ashbrook Center has become, in effect, a national university with unrivalled capacity for deepening teachers' understanding and appreciation of America.

The Ashbrook Center offers programs and resources to help citizens understand important public policy questions in the light of the principles and practice of constitutional self-government.

Visit us online at ashbrook.org TeachingAmericanHistory.org and OhioFarmer.org.